Collins

A REALLY BRITISH GUIDE TO MODERN ENGLISH

Tom Rees

Published by Collins
An imprint of HarperCollins Publishers
1 Robroyston Gate
Glasgow
G33 1JN

HarperCollins Publishers
Macken House, 39/40 Mayor Street Upper,
Dublin 1, D01 C9W8 Ireland

First Edition 2026
Previously published as *A Really British Guide to English* by *EAT SLEEP DREAM ENGLISH*

10 9 8 7 6 5 4 3 2 1

ISBN 978-0-00-881129-7

collins.co.uk/elt

Typeset by Davidson Publishing Solutions, Glasgow

Printed in India

A catalogue record for this book is available from the British Library.

If you would like to comment on any aspect of this book, please contact us at the given address or online.
E-mail: collins.elt@harpercollins.co.uk

Acknowledgements

AUTHOR
Tom Rees

ILLUSTRATOR
Javier Joaquín (Beehive Illustration)

DESIGNERS
James Hunter
Kevin Robbins

FOR THE PUBLISHER
Kerry Ferguson
Fiona McGlade
Mary O'Neill

WITH SPECIAL THANKS TO
Nikki Kipfmiller

FSC www.fsc.org
MIX
Paper | Supporting responsible forestry
FSC™ C016779

Contents

LET'S GET STARTED

INTRODUCTION

I've been British pretty much since the moment I was born. My mum used to say with pride that my first words were 'sorry!', 'chuffed' and 'I'd love a cuppa!'.

OK, that isn't strictly true, but I have been passionate about English for as long as I can remember.

I love how we use language to express our thoughts, feelings and opinions. We use it to make sense of the world around us and shape our own individual identity.

Each lexical choice we make is an expression of who we are and how we want people to perceive us.

In the UK, the following choices are powerful signifiers of your identity:

Do you say 'toilet' or 'little boy's room'?

Is it 'ay up' or 'how do you do'?

Would you order a 'cuppa' or a 'brew'?

The words you choose express who you are on so many levels. And this, to me, is the joy of language. A free space to assert your place in the world. After all, language is a dance, a dance we get to choreograph as we go. British English is so rich and playful – so please follow your curiosity and unearth all the lexical gems that await you in this book.

The purpose of *A Really British Guide to Modern English* is simple: to give you a fun, in-depth guide to British English and the culture that comes with it. Inside, you'll find linguistic treasures that will surprise and delight you. Many of them are integral parts of everyday British English, while others are more regional and niche. Other terms you come across might be a little old-fashioned or seen as derogatory or rude. My intention is not to teach these words for productive use, it's to bring enough focus to them so that you can understand the world around you. Sometimes, we might not realise the power of words in another language. We haven't grown up with them and we don't understand the weight they carry. With this in mind, I've flagged where language is slang or rude to give you some help and guidance. As a general point, the language in this book is mainly informal, and generally not intended to be used in formal, academic or professional settings.

At the heart of this book is one word: connection. Having lived and taught in different countries around the world, I've realised that's what languages give us. Connection to the people, culture and environment around us. My sincere hope is that this book helps, in some way, to connect you to the UK and makes you feel at home. Whether you've made a life for yourself in this country or you are just passing through, it's good to have you here.

Happy reading!

Tom Rees

ABOUT THE AUTHOR

Tom Rees is a London-based English educator and online content creator. He is the founder of Eat Sleep Dream English, a global platform helping students learn about the language and culture of the UK. His teaching career has taken him around the world, from Spain and Argentina to Hong Kong and the UK.

ACKNOWLEDGEMENTS

This book could not have been possible without a few special people. Firstly, I'd like to thank my Eat Sleep Dream English community of learners. I'm always humbled by how kind and supportive you all are. I hope this book becomes your trusty guide, helping you navigate the world around you and ultimately make you feel at home here in the UK.

I'd like to give a shout out to Fiona and Kerry at HarperCollins for putting their faith in me and helping this book come to life.

An enormous thank you to Luke Jones and Joe Edwards, my dear friends who both contributed to the making of this book and supported me from the word go.

I owe a huge debt of gratitude to my dad and sister for their ongoing love and support. They have been my sounding boards and my biggest cheerleaders throughout this journey.

They say the apple doesn't fall far from the tree, and for me, it all starts with my mum. She was the one who inspired me to become a teacher and author. Witnessing her love of the English language set me off on this journey in 2007. Sadly, she passed away in 2017, but everything I have accomplished since then has had her gentle influence. This is for you, Mum.

Finally, I'd like to give a very special thanks to my wife, Shana, for her knowledge, support and inspiration. She has been my anchor throughout this journey, helping me navigate the storms of business and life. I literally couldn't have done this without you.

HOW THIS BOOK WORKS

Here's a short guide to the different sections you'll find in the book.

A VERY SHORT GUIDE TO BRITAIN

We start the book with an overview of the geography, politics and religion of the UK. Who is the head of state? What is a British Overseas Territory? And what's the difference between the House of Commons and the House of Lords? All of these questions, and more, are answered here.

HOW TO SPEAK BRITISH

We then move on to our main section of the book: How to Speak British. Inside, you'll find a curated A–Z list of brilliant modern British English words, phrases, idioms, expressions and more. I've carefully selected the language Brits use in everyday life so that you can build a vocabulary that feels current, practical and instantly useful. As I explained in the Introduction, most of the language covered in the A–Z is informal, with some terms being labelled as slang or rude. This gives you the information you need to decide which words are appropriate for different contexts, and which words you might want to familiarise yourself with but not actually use.

Each entry in the A–Z section has:

- a word or phrase
- the part of speech: noun, adjective, etc.
- the IPA phonetic script to help with pronunciation (not for idioms and phrases)
- a slang or rude if it's needed
- the meaning
- an example sentence to put it into context.

Here's an example entry:

banger (noun) /ˈbæŋə/ slang
an informal word for a really great song.
'Have you heard the new Stormzy song?
It's an absolute banger!'

This is by no means an exhaustive list of all the words and phrases you'll come across in the UK, but it is a collection of the essentials. I want this book to reflect the English we really use in modern Britain. I've also peppered the list with 'Tom's Tips' to add a little cultural context, helpful insights and extra guidance along the way.

You can listen to audio recordings of the words and phrases in the A–Z at **collins.co.uk/eltresources**

You'll find two more mini-sections within this chapter: The first is 'What Brits Say and What They Actually Mean', which acts as a translation guide to help you decode the indirect, polite and often understated way Brits communicate – essential for anyone trying to navigate life in the UK successfully! The second is 'How to Pronounce Tricky UK Place Names'. Let's be honest, the pronunciation of place names in the UK can be a minefield for visitors (and Brits) so I've put together a little guide to help you say them like a local.

IT'S A LONDON THING

This section is all about the language of our capital city. We start with an insider's guide to Cockney rhyming slang, then move on to look at Modern London slang. The Modern London Slang A–Z showcases how contemporary English in the city has been heavily influenced by London's multicultural nature.

BRITISH VS WORLD ENGLISH

We move on to celebrate the influences of the world on British English. We start by comparing and contrasting British English with American English. Do you turn on a 'tap' or 'faucet'? Do you play 'football' or 'soccer'? Would you walk along a 'pavement' or 'sidewalk'? This section is here to help you figure it out.

After that, we look at the languages that have shaped modern British English, exploring how centuries of history, migration and cultural exchange have influenced the words we use today.

BRITISH ACCENTS

Our next chapter explores the main accents of the UK. This is your chance to identify the differences between the main regional varieties and get answers to the big questions like:

How many accents are there in the UK?

Does everyone speak like the King?

How do Brits really say 'bottle of water'?

We begin with seven prominent accents from England: Received Pronunciation, Cockney, Multicultural London English, Scouse, Mancunian, Geordie and Brummie. For each one, I break down the key pronunciation features and provide an example sentence along with an audio example so you can hear it in action. We then move on to look at pronunciation features found in Scotland, Wales and Northern Ireland, so you get a broader understanding of the sounds you'll hear there.

You can listen to audio recordings of the example sentences from this chapter at **collins.co.uk/eltresources**

PRACTICE

Finally, it's time to put everything into practice and consolidate what you've learned throughout the book. The last activity is 'The Great British Quiz' — perfect for a classroom test or a fun family quiz night.

Ultimately, this book is designed to give you the English you need to understand the world around you, so when you are ready, let's begin!

A VERY SHORT GUIDE TO BRITAIN

POPULATION: 68 million
CAPITAL: London

GEOGRAPHY

Let's start with the basics. What is the difference between the UK, Britain, England, etc.?

The United Kingdom of Great Britain and Northern Ireland (**United Kingdom** or **UK** for short) – a sovereign state made up of four constituent countries: **England**, **Scotland**, **Wales** and **Northern Ireland**.

Great Britain – a geographical term for the island that includes three countries: England, Scotland and Wales.

Britain – this term can cause confusion, as it can be used to mean both the island of Great Britain and the country of the United Kingdom.

The British Isles – a geographical term for Great Britain, the island of Ireland, the Isle of Man, Orkney, Shetland and the Channel Islands.

Commonwealth realms – sovereign states within the Commonwealth that recognise the UK monarch as their head of state. There are 15 in total, including Canada, Australia, New Zealand, Papua New Guinea and Jamaica.

British Overseas Territories – often also called United Kingdom Overseas Territories – 14 territories that are located outside the territorial waters of the UK. Each one runs its own affairs to different degrees, but they all recognise the King as head of state. Some examples are Bermuda, the Cayman Islands, Gibraltar, the Falkland Islands and the British Virgin Islands.

Crown Dependencies – the self-governing territories of Guernsey, Jersey and the Isle of Man are not part of the United Kingdom, though the UK is responsible for certain areas such as defence and international relations. All three recognise the UK monarch as head of state.

POLITICS

King Charles III is the head of state for the United Kingdom but holds no political influence. As such, it is the Prime Minister, as the Head of Government, who has the most political authority. The UK has a parliamentary government that meets in the Palace of Westminster (also known as the Houses of Parliament) in London. There are two main houses: the elected House of Commons and the unelected House of Lords. The three most established political parties are the Labour Party, the Conservative Party and the Liberal Democrats. Each country also has its own parties; for example, the Scottish National Party (SNP) in Scotland, Plaid Cymru in Wales and the Democratic Unionist Party and Sinn Féin in Northern Ireland. The UK has a fixed-term parliament, which states that a general election must be held on the first Thursday of May, five years after the previous election, although an election can be called before then if required.

Scotland, Wales and Northern Ireland all have their own governments, which make decisions on matters such as education, healthcare and local government. London has also had an assembly and a mayor since 2000.

RELIGION

Although a significant proportion of the United Kingdom's population doesn't identify with any religion, the UK can best be described as a multi-faith society in which Christianity is the largest religion, with Protestant denominations forming the largest Christian grouping. England has an established church, the Church of England, while Scotland's national church is the Church of Scotland. Wales and Northern Ireland have no established church. There are also large communities of people who follow Catholicism, Islam, Judaism, Hinduism and Sikhism. Because of this huge diversity, you can find communities observing all the major religious festivals throughout the year.

HOW TO SPEAK BRITISH

A–Z OF BRITISH VOCABULARY

A

A&E (noun) /eɪ ən ˈiː/
the accident and emergency department in a hospital.
'A&E departments have been pushed to breaking point this winter.'

a bit of (me) (phrase) slang
used to say you like something or are interested in it.
'Coldplay are a bit of me.'

a bit on the side (idiom)
a romantic or physical relationship with someone who isn't your primary partner.
'Two years into their marriage he found out she had a bit on the side with a colleague.'

ace (adjective) /eɪs/
really good.
'Throwing Miko a surprise birthday party is an ace idea guys, well done!'

across the pond (phrase) slang
an informal term for the other side of the Atlantic Ocean.
'So many bands have found it hard to go across the pond and be as successful as they are in the UK.'

afternoon tea (noun) /ɑːftənuːn ˈtiː/
a meal in the afternoon, usually consisting of tea, sandwiches, scones and cakes.
'My mother and I make a tradition of going for afternoon tea every year for her birthday.'

afters (noun) /ˈɑːftəz/
another word for 'dessert'.
'What do you kids want for afters? I've got ice cream or jelly.'

afters (noun) /ˈɑːftəz/ slang
the continuation of aggression between people after the main confrontation. Often used between sports players immediately after they have been involved in a challenge for the ball.
'There was a bit of afters between the goalkeeper and opposition striker.'

after the Lord Mayor's show (idiom)
an anti-climatic or disappointing event that comes straight after an exciting one.
'Last week's cup final was so exciting, today's game was always going to feel a little bit like after the Lord Mayor's show.'

aggro (noun) /ˈæɡrəʊ/
short for ‘aggression’.
‘*There was a lot of aggro at the football yesterday.*’

agony aunt (noun) /ˈæɡəni ɑːnt/
a person, traditionally a woman, who offers advice to people via a magazine or newspaper column, and nowadays on many online platforms.
‘*I’ve never written in to an agony aunt but I’d be tempted if I had a serious problem.*’

‘airy-fairy’

airy-fairy (adjective) /ˈeəri ˈfeəri/
a disapproving term describing something that is vague and impractical.
‘*All these business ideas are a bit airy-fairy.*’

alcopop (noun) /ˈælkəʊpɒp/
a type of fizzy alcoholic drink that usually comes in fruity flavours.
‘*All we ever drank at uni was alcopops.*’

A-levels (noun) /ˈeɪ levəlz/
Advanced-level qualifications in certain subjects, taken by students usually aged 16–18 in the UK (except for Scotland). Students take A-levels after doing GCSEs.
‘*My daughter is planning to take five A-levels next year.*’

all mouth (and no trousers) (phrase)
slang
a phrase that describes someone who talks a lot about doing something, but never backs it up with action.
‘*Sven keeps saying he’s going to sign up for the London marathon, but I suspect he’s all mouth and no trousers.*’

allotment (noun) /əˈlɒtmənt/
a small plot of land that is owned by the local council but rented to individuals to grow their own plants and vegetables.
‘*My grandma has had an allotment by the canal for over 30 years.*’

all over the (shop/gaff/place) (phrase)
slang
an informal phrase for ‘disorganised’.
A – ‘How was the game?’
B – ‘Terrible! We lost 5–0! The team was all over the shop from the first minute.’

alright! (exclamation) /ɔːlˈraɪt/
a common informal way to say ‘hello’.
‘*Alright Jack, how’s it going?*’

an arm and a leg (idiom)
if something costs an arm and a leg, it’s very expensive.
‘*Flights to Dubai cost an arm and a leg right now.*’

Angel of the North (noun) /eɪndʒəl əv ðə ˈnɔːθ/
a magnificent steel sculpture of an angel, created by Anthony Gormley, that measures 20 metres high and stands just outside Gateshead in the northeast of England.
‘*If you take the train from London to Edinburgh, you pass the Angel of the North just before coming into Newcastle.*’

anorak (noun) /ˈænəræk/
a jacket that is worn to protect you from rain and wind.
‘*It’s lucky we brought our anoraks. It looks like it’s going to rain very soon.*’

anorak (noun) /ˈænəræk/
someone who is really interested in a hobby that most people think is boring.
'My uncle is a big transport anorak. He loves collecting the serial numbers of trains that he's ridden on.'

anyroad (adverb) /ˈenirəʊd/
a word used in the north of England instead of 'anyway'.
'It's too late to go to the party, and anyroad I've got nowt to wear.'

argy-bargy (noun) /ˈɑːdʒi ˈbɑːdʒi/
loud verbal disagreement that can sometimes become physical.
'There was some argy-bargy at the match so we left early.'

arse (noun) /ɑːs/ rude
slang for 'bottom'.
'Does my arse look big in these jeans?'

arsehole (noun) /ˈɑːshəʊl/ rude
a vulgar word for a person's anus. It's also used as an offensive word for someone you think is stupid or contemptible.
'Anjali's boyfriend has been acting like a complete arsehole recently. I wish she'd dump him.'

arse over tit (phrase) rude
if you go arse over tit, you fall over in a dramatic and uncontrolled way.
'We went ice-skating last weekend and as soon as my father-in-law got on the ice, he went arse over tit.'

arty-farty (adjective) /ˈɑːti ˈfɑːti/
a disapproving term for someone or something trying too hard to be cool and arty. It's similar to 'pretentious'.
'Simone is out with her arty-farty friends tonight, so I'm staying in and watching a film.'

(The) Ashes (noun) /ˈæʃɪz/
a test cricket series played between England and Australia.
'Australia completely outplayed England in the Ashes this year.'

at a loose end (idiom)
having nothing to do.
'I'm at a bit of a loose end this afternoon. Do you fancy doing something?'

at His (or Her) Majesty's pleasure (euphemism)
detained in prison.
'My uncle has been at His Majesty's pleasure for as long as I can remember.'

Auld Reekie (noun) /ɔːld ˈriːki/
a nickname for Edinburgh.
'Auld Reekie means "old smoky" in the Scots language.'

autumn (noun) /ˈɔːtəm/
the season between summer and winter (September–November UK).
'Autumn is a beautiful season here, particularly when the leaves change colour.'

'ave it (phrase) slang
used to encourage someone to do something (short for 'have it'). Made famous by comedian Peter Kay in an advert for John Smith's beer.
'Come on lads, let's 'ave it!'

aye (exclamation) /aɪ/
used to say 'yes', particularly in the north of England and in Scotland.
A – 'Are you coming to the party, Rob?'
B – 'Aye, I'll be there.'

ay up (phrase)
a greeting used mostly in the north of England and the East Midlands to replace 'hello' or 'hi'.
'Ay up love, how's your day going?'

B

bab (noun) /bæb/
an affectionate term used primarily in the Midlands and north of England.
'Come here bab, you look like you need a hug.'

babes (noun) /beɪbz/
an affectionate term particularly prevalent in Essex and southeast England.
'Babes, are you coming to my hen party next month?'

baccy (noun) /ˈbæki/ slang
tobacco that can be rolled to make cigarettes.
'Can I borrow some baccy? I fancy a quick cigarette before work.'

backbencher (noun) /bækˈbentʃə/
an elected Member of Parliament who is not in the cabinet. They are called this because they sit on the benches behind the front bench, which holds the cabinet or shadow cabinet.
'Several backbenchers rebelled against the government in the latest vote.'

backhander (noun) /bækˈhændə/
if you give someone a backhander, you give them a bribe, i.e. a secret illegal payment.
'It is reported that the government was receiving backhanders from construction companies to get big contracts.'

BAFTA (noun) /ˈbæftə/
British Academy of Film and Television Arts. A British organisation that supports art forms such as film, television and gaming in the United Kingdom.
'The BAFTA awards are some of the most important in the world for filmmakers.'

bagsy (verb) /ˈbægzi/
to guarantee the right to do or have something. A playful word commonly used by children.
'At nursery, I would always bagsy the big blue chair before anyone else.'

'bagsy'

bairn (noun) /beən/
a Scottish term for a baby or child.
'Your wee bairn is so cute. How old is she?'

baked beans (noun) /beɪkt ˈbiːnz/
in Britain, these are white beans in a tomato sauce, usually sold in tins, and served as part of a British breakfast or on toast.
'All I've got in my cupboard is a few tins of baked beans and a packet of instant noodles.'

balls (something) up (phrasal verb) /bɔːlz ˈʌp/ rude
a slang term meaning to make a mistake or do something stupid.
'I managed to balls up my driving test three times before I passed.'

Balmoral Castle (noun) /bælˈmɒrəl ˈkɑ:səl/
the private estate in Scotland, owned by the King. It's one of his many residences.
'The King is spending the summer at Balmoral Castle.'

balti (noun) /ˈbɔ:lti/
a style of curry served in a metal dish, originating in Birmingham. There is an area called the Balti Triangle in the south of the city, which has a large number of Balti houses.
'Let's go check out the Balti Triangle when we visit your cousin.'

baltic (adjective) /ˈbɔ:ltɪk/
extremely cold.
'It's absolutely baltic outside.'

bang (verb) /bæŋ/ rude slang
to have sex with someone.
'How many people have you banged in your life?'

banger (noun) /ˈbæŋə/ slang
an informal word for a really great song.
'Have you heard the new Stormzy song? It's an absolute banger!'

banger (noun) /ˈbæŋə/
an informal word for a sausage.
'Kids, we are having bangers and mash for dinner, is that OK?'

banger (noun) /ˈbæŋə/ slang
an old car in bad condition.
'I'm sick of driving an old banger, I'm desperate to get myself something new.'

bang on (phrase)
exactly right.
A – 'The problem with the NHS is the lack of funding.'
B – 'You're bang on!'

bang on (about something) (phrase)
to talk about something for so long it becomes boring or annoying to the listener (you can replace 'bang' with 'go').
'Kofi wouldn't stop banging on about how great his new job is.'

bang out of order (phrase) slang
if someone does something that is bang out of order, it is not appropriate, cool or reasonable.
'What you said to Sachin was bang out of order. You should go and apologise immediately!'

bang tidy (adjective) /ˈbæŋ taɪdi/ slang
very attractive.
'Have you seen Megan's new girlfriend? She's bang tidy if you ask me.'

bang to rights (phrase)
with enough evidence to prove that someone is guilty of a crime.
'He literally had blood on his hands so the police had him bang to rights.'

bank holiday (noun) /bæŋk ˈhɒlɪdeɪ/
a public holiday in the United Kingdom.
'Are you going away for the bank holiday weekend?'

banter (noun) /ˈbæntə/
teasing playful conversation, usually between people that know each other. It can involve gentle mocking or teasing (often shortened to 'bants').
'There's always a lot of banter between my colleagues at work.'

barking mad (adjective) /ˈbɑ:kɪŋ mæd/ slang
a disapproving term meaning completely irrational, foolish, or acting very strangely.
'You'd be barking mad to quit your job right now.'

'Barmy Army'

barm cake (noun) /ˈbɑːm keɪk/
a bread bun, used in some parts of the north of England.
'I'll get us a couple of barm cakes for lunch.'

barmy (adjective) /ˈbɑːmi/ slang
a term for 'crazy'. It can be used positively or negatively for someone or something depending on the context.
'You want to go to Oxford Street on a Saturday afternoon! Are you barmy?'

Barmy Army (noun) /ˈbɑːmi ˈɑːmi/
a name given to a large group of fans that follow the England cricket team.
'The Barmy Army have been singing all afternoon here at Lord's.'

barney (noun) /ˈbɑːni/ slang
a fight or argument.
'I've just had a huge barney with my flatmate about cleaning the toilet.'

barrister (noun) /ˈbærɪstə/
a senior lawyer in the United Kingdom who can argue cases in higher courts.
'My niece is training to be a barrister.'

bawbag (noun) /ˈbɔːbæg/ rude
a Scottish slang term for 'scrotum' that can also be used as a derogatory term for a useless person.
'My boss just fired three staff for being late. He's such a bawbag!'

BBC (noun) /biː biː ˈsiː/
the British Broadcasting Corporation is a television and radio organisation (also known as 'the Beeb').
'My sister worked for the BBC for ten years.'

beastly (adjective) /ˈbiːstli/
an old-fashioned word meaning 'unpleasant'.
'I don't understand why my boss is being so beastly to me today.'

Bedfordshire (noun) /ˈbedfədʃɪə/
a humorous and not very commonly used alternative for 'bed'. It was most notably used by Bridget Jones.
'OK guys, I'm off to Bedfordshire. See you all in the morning.'

bedsit (noun) /ˈbedsɪt/
a single room where someone lives, with sleeping and cooking facilities.
'I lived in a bedsit in Notting Hill for ten years before I was able to buy a one-bed flat in Hammersmith.'

Beefeater (noun) /ˈbiːfiːtə/
the informal term for a ceremonial guard of the Tower of London. They wear ornate red and black uniforms and are formally known as Yeomen Warders.
'I'm very proud to say my grandfather was a Beefeater for over 30 years.'

beer monster (noun) /ˈbɪə mɒnstə/ slang
someone who can drink a huge amount of beer.
'The uni rugby team are absolute beer monsters.'

bell-end (noun) /ˈbel end/ rude
a slang term for a penis. Also used as a very rude insult for someone stupid or contemptible.
'Look at that guy trying to fight the bouncers. What a bell-end!'

belter (noun) /ˈbeltə/ slang
something that is excellent.
A – 'How was your weekend?'
B – 'It was an absolute belter.'

belting (adjective) /ˈbeltɪŋ/ slang
an informal word for 'wonderful' or 'excellent'.
'I've had a belting birthday so far guys, thanks so much for making me feel so special.'

belt up (phrasal verb) /ˈbelt ʌp/ slang
an informal rude way to say 'shut up'.
'I was shocked when Maria told her kids to belt up! I'd never speak to my children like that.'

bender (noun) /ˈbendə/ slang
a wild drinking session.
'For Matt's stag party we went on a two-day bender. I've never felt so ill afterwards.'

bent (adjective) /bent/ slang
dishonest.
'Did you read the story about two bent coppers who were stealing money from pensioners?'

berk (noun) /bɜːk/ slang
an old-fashioned insult for someone, similar to 'idiot'.
'Why is that berk trying to park in a bus lane?'

best-before date (noun) /best bɪˈfɔː deɪt/
the date printed on food that shows consumers when the product should be consumed. After this date, the food is still edible, but the quality becomes worse.
'The best-before date on this cheese was a week ago!'

bevvy (noun) /ˈbevi/ slang
an alcoholic drink.
'I went for a few bevvies with Mark after work.'

bezzie (noun) /ˈbezi/
an informal way to say best friend (also 'bestie' and 'bezzie mate').
'Isla and Saffy have been bezzies for years.'

bickie (noun) /ˈbɪki/
short for 'biscuit'.
'Do you want a bickie with your tea?'

TOM'S TIPS

Britain is a bickie-loving nation. Our favourites include chocolate digestives, Hobnobs, rich teas, custard creams and ginger nuts. And if you want to start a debate with a British person, simply ask them if they think Jaffa Cakes are biscuits or cakes... This question divides the country.

bifter (noun) /ˈbɪftə/ slang
a cigarette (usually containing cannabis).
'Let's roll a bifter for the walk home.'

big girl's blouse (idiom)
an old-fashioned insult to describe a cowardly man.
A – 'I think you've broken my finger.'
B – 'Don't be such a big girl's blouse. I barely touched you!'

bint (noun) /bɪnt/ rude
an offensive insult for a woman.
'Please don't call anyone a bint, it's terribly rude.'

bird (noun) /bɜːd/ slang
a very informal word for a woman. It can be seen as offensive.
'I hope there are loads of hot birds at the party tonight.'

'bingo wings'

Billy no-mates (phrase) slang
someone who doesn't have any friends.
'Both my flatmates are away at the moment, so I'm Billy no-mates for the weekend.'

bingo wings (noun) /ˈbɪŋgəʊ wɪŋz/ slang
a very informal phrase that describes the loose skin that hangs down from someone's upper arm as they wave. The saying originates from old overweight ladies raising their arms as they shout 'bingo' in the bingo halls of Britain.
'I've joined a gym because I want to get rid of my bingo wings.'

bin man (noun) /ˈbɪn mæn/
someone who collects the rubbish. These days it's more correct to say 'refuse collector'.
'My dad used to be a bin man after he left school.'

bin off (phrasal verb) /bɪn ˈɒf/ slang
to end a relationship (mostly used in the north of England).
'Did you hear Clara binned off Timmy and has started dating a new guy?'

bish bash bosh (phrase)
a phrase used to indicate something has been completed quickly or without fuss.
'Add your eggs, flour, sugar and chocolate, and bish bash bosh you've got your cake.'

bits and bobs (noun) /bɪts ən ˈbɒbz/
small objects or miscellaneous things. We often use it when it would take too long naming all the things or when we don't know the words for them.
'I'm just going to buy some bits and bobs from Tesco.'

black pudding (noun) /blæk ˈpʊdɪŋ/
a type of blood sausage made with pig's blood, oatmeal and fat. It's most commonly eaten as part of a full English breakfast.
'Black pudding is an acquired taste.'

blag (verb) /blæg/ slang
to use cunning, smarts or dishonesty to get something you want from someone, e.g. getting into a concert without tickets or getting a free coffee.
'My cousin once blagged his way into a Prince concert.'

blag artist (noun) /ˈblæg ɑ:tɪst/ slang
someone who is extremely good at getting what they want using cunning or slight dishonesty (also 'blagger').
'I can't believe how much free stuff Jenny gets. She is such a blag artist.'

'blimey!'

blank (someone) (verb) /blæŋk/
to ignore someone deliberately.
'Oh my goodness! Did you just blank your ex-boyfriend?'

blast (noun) /blɑ:st/
a good time.
'We had such a blast at your party, thanks so much for inviting us.'

blast! (exclamation) /blɑ:st/
used to express annoyance or frustration.
'Blast! I accidentally threw away the receipt for this jacket and now I can't return it.'

bleeding (adjective) /ˈbli:dɪŋ/ slang
used to emphasise something. Often used in negative situations.
'That bleeding car's broken down again!'

bleeding (adverb) /ˈbli:dɪŋ/ slang
used as an intensifier to emphasise something in a negative way.
'That mattress is bleeding heavy. I'm going to need a hand carrying it up the stairs.'

blighter (noun) /ˈblaɪtə/ slang
an old-fashioned term for a person you see as irritating or you have pity for.
'Look at those poor blighters outside getting wet in the rain.'

Blighty (noun) /ˈblaɪti/
an old-fashioned nickname for Britain or England, often used by British people abroad. The first citations are from the Boer War and it was often used by soldiers in the First and Second World Wars.
'They haven't been home to Blighty since they were children.'

blimey! (exclamation) /ˈblaɪmi/
used to show surprise.
'Blimey! I didn't realise this film was three hours long.'

blinder (noun) /ˈblaɪndə/ slang
an excellent performance (also 'play a blinder').
'Rory McIlroy played a blinder at the Ryder Cup.'

blinding (adjective) /ˈblaɪndɪŋ/ slang
excellent.
'Stan had a blinding game and scored two goals in ten minutes.'

block of flats (noun) /blɒk əv ˈflæts/
a large building made up of flats.
'She grew up in a block of flats in Hackney.'

bloke (noun) /bləʊk/ slang
an informal word for a man.
'Kwan is such a lovely bloke.'

bloody (adjective) /ˈblʌdi/ rude
used to express anger.
'You're acting like a bloody idiot!'

bloody (adverb) /ˈblʌdi/ rude
used as an intensifier to emphasise something in a rude way.
'Goodness me, that personal trainer is bloody useless. He has no idea what he's doing.'

bloody hell (phrase) rude
used to show anger or annoyance.
'Bloody hell! There's a stain on the new carpet.'

blooming (adjective) /ˈbluːmɪŋ/
used to express anger or annoyance.
'Today has been a blooming disaster!'

blooming (adverb) /ˈbluːmɪŋ/
used to emphasise something.
'It's a blooming long way to walk. Are you sure you don't want to take a taxi?'

blower (noun) /ˈbləʊə/ slang
an informal word for 'telephone'.
'Raheem has been on the blower with his girlfriend for hours.'

blue (noun) /bluː/
a term given to someone who has played sport for Oxford or Cambridge University against the other university.
'Sally became an Oxford blue when she rowed in the boat race last year.'

bob (noun) /bɒb/ slang
an informal word used these days to describe an indefinite amount of money. It comes from when Britain used a pre-decimal system. Back then, a 'bob' was the slang term for a shilling coin.
'Have you got a few bob I can give to the carol singers when they come round?'

bobbins (adjective) /ˈbɒbɪnz/
not very good, not true or worthless.
'My mobile is absolute bobbins! It doesn't even make calls anymore.'

bobble hat (noun) /ˈbɒbəl hæt/
a hat made of wool with a small wool ball on top, usually worn in winter.
'My gran made me this bobble hat for Christmas.'

bobby (noun) /ˈbɒbi/ slang
an old-fashioned word for a police officer.
'You don't see so many bobbies on the street these days.'

Bob's your uncle (idiom)
used to say 'there it is' or 'and it's done'. Often used to show how easy it is to do a task.
'You put all the ingredients in a bowl, stir them together and Bob's your uncle, you've got the most delicious salad.'

bog (noun) /bɒg/ slang
a toilet.
'Do you want to use the bog before we head out?'

bogey (noun) /ˈbəʊgi/ slang
a dried, hardened piece of mucus found inside one's nose.
'Mate, you've got a bogey hanging out of your nose!'

bog roll (noun) /ˈbɒg rəʊl/ slang
toilet paper.
'Can you buy some bog roll on your way home?'

bog-standard (adjective) /bɒg ˈstændəd/
average and not very special.
A – 'What kind of TV did you buy?'
B – 'Nothing special, just a bog-standard one.'

bollard (noun) /ˈbɒlɑːd/
a short post used to stop cars from entering a designated area.
'They put a load of bollards across Maltby Street so cars can't go down it anymore.'

bollocking (noun) /ˈbɒləkɪŋ/ rude
a rude term for telling someone off or reprimanding them in a very strong, angry way.
'Our rugby coach gave us an absolute bollocking after we lost the game by five tries.'

bollocks (noun) /ˈbɒləks/ rude
a slang term for a man's testicles.
'There is nothing more painful for a guy than getting hit in the bollocks.'

bollocks! (exclamation) /ˈbɒləks/ rude
used to show frustration, anger or disagreement.
'Oh bollocks! I've left my phone charger in the cafe.'

bonce (noun) /bɒns/ slang
your head.
'Do you want to borrow a cap to cover your bonce? The sun is super strong today.'

Bonfire Night (noun) /ˈbɒnfaɪə naɪt/
A celebration on 5th November when British people light bonfires and fireworks to remember the Gunpowder Plot to blow up the Houses of Parliament by Guy Fawkes in 1605. It's also called Guy Fawkes Night.
'There are huge fireworks displays all across the country on Bonfire Night.'

bonk (verb) /bɒŋk/ rude slang
to have sex.
'The newly married couple bonked as soon as they were on honeymoon.'

bonkers (adjective) /ˈbɒŋkəz/ slang
very silly, or acting in a crazy way.
'The stock market is absolutely bonkers at the moment.'

bonnet (noun) /ˈbɒnɪt/
the metal cover that goes over the engine in a car.
'Lift the bonnet up and let's have a look at the engine.'

bonny (adjective) /ˈbɒni/
a Scottish word meaning 'beautiful' and 'healthy'. Also used in the northeast of England.
'My cousin has just had a bonny little baby girl called Emilia.'

(the) bookies (phrase) slang
a betting shop, short for 'bookmaker'.
'Let's pop down to the bookies and place a bet on the Grand National.'

boot (noun) /buːt/
the compartment at the back of a car where you generally put luggage or objects to transport.
'Shall I put the bags in the boot?'

'Bonfire Night'

booze (noun) /buːz/ slang
alcohol.
'I haven't had any booze since January.'

boozer (noun) /ˈbuːzə/ slang
a pub. It can also be a slang term for someone who drinks a lot.
'There's a great little boozer next to Farringdon station.'

boozy (adjective) /ˈbuːzi/
containing or drinking lots of alcohol.
'We had a really boozy night out on Thursday last week.'

Boris bike (noun) /ˈbɒris baɪk/
a colloquial name for the public bike-hire scheme in London. It's named after Boris Johnson, who was the Mayor of London when the scheme launched in 2010.
'The quickest way to get to Old Street is probably on a Boris bike.'

boss (adjective) /bɒs/ slang
very good, heard mostly in the northwest of England.
'Your trainers are boss! Where did you get them from?'

boss-eyed (adjective) /ˈbɒs aɪd/ slang
having eyes that seem to look in towards each other (also 'cross-eyed').
'I've been staring at a screen for so long I think I've gone boss-eyed.'

bosting (adjective) /ˈbɒstiŋ/ slang
very good (used in the Midlands).
'Have a bostin' holiday, Abi.'

botch job (noun) /ˈbɒtʃ dʒɒb/
a piece of work that is badly done.
'I asked my plumber to fix my taps, but he did a complete botch job and made things worse.'

bottle (noun) /ˈbɒtəl/ slang
courage.
'I'd love to be a stand-up comedian, but I don't have the bottle to get up on stage.'

bottle it (phrase) slang
to not do something because you don't have the courage.
'I was going to ask him on a date during our lunch break, but I completely bottled it.'

bouncer (noun) /ˈbaʊnsə/
someone employed by a nightclub or pub to protect the customers and stop trouble from happening, such as fighting or drug dealing, etc.
'The bouncers at Equinox are really strict about who can enter.'

bouncy castle (noun) /baʊnsi ˈkɑːsəl/
a large inflatable object filled with air that children (or adults) can jump and play on.
'We've hired a bouncy castle for Rafa's birthday party.'

Boxing Day (noun) /ˈbɒksɪŋ deɪ/
the day after Christmas Day.
'We always go and visit my cousins on Boxing Day.'

boyo (noun) /ˈbɔɪəʊ/ slang
a Welsh term of address for a boy or man.
'Alright boyo, fancy coming to the rugby with me and your uncle on Sunday?'

boy's a dear (phrase)
used in Northern Ireland to react to bad news.
A – 'Our landlord has asked us to move out.'
B – 'Boy's a dear!'

brassic (adjective) /ˈbræsɪk/ slang
if someone is brassic, they have no money (also 'boracic').
'I'm totally brassic till the end of the month.'

brass neck (noun) /brɑ:s ˈnek/
someone with a brass neck is confident to say or do whatever they want, but who doesn't understand that their behaviour isn't acceptable to other people.
'She's got a brass neck asking me for money when she still owes me £1,000.'

bread and butter (noun) /bred ən ˈbʌtə/
the job that gives you your main income.
'My job at the accountancy firm is my bread and butter while I retrain to become a landscape gardener.'

brew (noun) /bru:/ slang
a cup of tea. Mostly used in the north of England.
'I'd love a brew if you are going to make one.'

Brexit (noun) /ˈbreksɪt/
the withdrawal of the United Kingdom from the European Union.
'Brexit is still a very divisive issue for people in the UK.'

Brexiteer (noun) /breksɪˈtɪə/
someone who voted for and supports the United Kingdom's exit from the European Union.
'Some of the most vocal Brexiteers were Boris Johnson and Jacob Rees-Mogg.'

brick it (idiom) slang
to feel nervous or scared.
'I was bricking it before my driving test.'

brill (adjective) /brɪl/
a short form of 'brilliant'.
A – 'Annie and Stew said they can come to the wedding!'
B – 'Brill!'

Bristolian (noun) /brɪˈstəʊliən/
a native of Bristol.
'I love the way Bristolians speak.'

Brit (noun) /brɪt/
a short word for a British person.
'There are hundreds of thousands of Brits who go on holiday to the south of Spain every year.'

Brizzle (noun) /ˈbrɪzəl/ slang
an affectionate word for the city of Bristol.
'My cousins live in Brizzle.'

'I love Brizzle!'

brolly (noun) /ˈbrɒli/
an informal word for 'umbrella'.
'Damn! I forgot my brolly and it's pouring with rain outside.'

Brum (noun) /brʌm/
an affectionate term for the city of Birmingham.
'We are having a uni reunion in Brum this summer.'

Brummie (noun) /ˈbrʌmi/
someone from Birmingham. It's also the name of the accent of the city (also 'Brummy').
'Brummies are very proud of their city.'

bruv (noun) /brʌv/ slang
a short form of 'brother'. Used to greet a male, similar to 'mate'.
'Bruv, when is your birthday?'

BST (abbreviation) /biː es ˈtiː/
British Summer Time.
'Our meeting will be at 3 p.m. BST.'

bubble and squeak (noun) /bʌbəl ən ˈskwiːk/
a type of food that is made from leftovers – usually potato and cabbage – and then fried in a pan. It's often served with a full English breakfast.
'Do you want bubble and squeak with your brekky, guys?'

buck's fizz (noun) /bʌks ˈfɪz/
an alcoholic drink made with orange juice and champagne.
'Would you like a buck's fizz with your brunch?'

budge up (phrasal verb) /bʌdʒ ˈʌp/
to move to make space for someone.
'If we all budge up a bit, Katie can sit on the bench too.'

buff (adjective) /bʌf/ slang
attractive.
'How buff is the new waiter at Morito?'

bugger! (exclamation) /ˈbʌgə/ rude
a vulgar word used to show frustration, anger or annoyance.
'Oh bugger! I've forgotten to bring my phone charger. Can I borrow yours?'

bugger all (phrase) rude
a vulgar way to say 'nothing'.
'We went on a whale-watching trip in Patagonia and saw bugger all!'

buggered (adjective) /ˈbʌgəd/ rude
a vulgar way to say 'broken'.
'My TV is buggered! Can I come round and watch Strictly Come Dancing at yours?'

builder's (tea/brew) (noun) /ˈbɪldəz/
a strong cup of English breakfast tea.
'I'll have a mug of builder's tea and some toast, please.'

building society (noun)
/ˈbɪldɪŋ səˈsaɪəti/
a building society is similar to a bank in the products it offers, but unlike a bank, which has shareholders and customers, a building society has members who can influence decisions the organisation makes.
'When I was a kid, my aunt set up an account for me at the local building society.'

built like a brick shithouse (phrase) rude
an impolite humorous phrase to describe someone who is really big and strong.
'Daisy's new boyfriend is built like a brick shithouse.'

bum (noun) /bʌm/
an informal word for a person's bottom.
'Every time I go ice-skating I manage to fall on my bum at least five times.'

bumbag (noun) /ˈbʌmbæg/
a small bag that wraps around the waist.
'I saw a guy with a BTS bumbag in Shoreditch today.'

bung (noun) /bʌŋ/ slang
a payment made to persuade someone to do something, usually illegally.
'Half the cricket team took bungs in order to lose the match.'

bunged-up (adjective) /bʌŋd ˈʌp/
if you are bunged-up, your nose is congested, which makes it hard to smell or breathe. It is usually a symptom of a cold.
'You sound a little bunged-up, Marco. Are you feeling alright?'

bunk off (phrasal verb) /ˈbʌŋk ɒf/ slang
to take time off school or work without permission.
'Did you know that your son bunked off school this morning, Mrs Plumb?'

Burns Night (noun) /ˈbɜːnz naɪt/
a festival that celebrates the life of the famous Scottish poet Robert Burns.
'We've having a special Burns Night supper if you'd like to join us.'

busker (noun) /ˈbʌskə/
someone who plays music in the street for money.
'When you walk around central London you'll hear some really good buskers.'

butters (adjective) /ˈbʌtəz/ slang
disgusting or unattractive.
'Oh my days, that dress is butters!'

butty (noun) /ˈbʌti/ slang
a term used mostly in the north of England for 'sandwich'.
'Can I get a chip butty and a can of coke, please?'

buzzing (adjective) /ˈbʌzɪŋ/ slang
excited or euphoric.
'The girls are buzzing to be going to Disneyland next week.'

by-election (noun) /ˈbaɪ ɪlekʃən/
an election to choose an MP who is replacing a politician who has quit or died during their time in parliament.
'Labour suffered an embarrassing defeat in the latest by-elections.'

by gum! (exclamation) /baɪ ˈgʌm/
an old-fashioned way to express surprise. Used mostly in the north of England.
'By gum! I think I just saw a snake in the garden.'

C

cabbie (noun) /ˈkæbi/ slang
a taxi driver.
'My uncle has been a cabbie for 30 years.'

cabinet (noun) /ˈkæbɪnɪt/
the cabinet is a decision-making body led by the Prime Minister and includes the 21 most-senior elected ministers in the UK government, known individually as cabinet ministers.
'The cabinet met on Friday afternoon to discuss the new trade proposals.'

caff (noun) /kæf/ slang
a type of restaurant that serves simple home-cooked food like English breakfasts at affordable prices. The decor is usually very basic and traditionally they have been an important part of the local community (also 'greasy spoon').
'There's a great little caff in Stepney Green that I've been going to for years.'

cakehole (noun) /ˈkeɪkhəʊl/ slang
your mouth.
'It's about time you shut your cakehole and started listening to other people's opinions.'

cannae (verb) /ˈkæni/
a Scottish form of 'can't'.
'Speak up Mum, I cannae hear you very well.'

canny (adjective) /ˈkæni/
nice or pleasant (used in Scotland and the north of England).
'My new neighbour seems like a canny lad.'

can't be arsed (phrase) rude
an expression to say that someone doesn't want to do something or doesn't have the energy to do it. It's a ruder version of 'can't be bothered'.
'I really can't be arsed to go to work today.'

can't be doing (with something) (phrase)
if you can't be doing with something, you don't have the patience or desire to deal with it.
'I can't be doing with all his nonsense. If he wants to stay together he needs to show me that he cares about this relationship.'

capital (adjective) /ˈkæpɪtəl/
an old-fashioned way to say 'excellent'.
'That's an absolutely capital plan guys.'

caravan (noun) /ˈkærəvæn/
a vehicle, pulled by a car, in which people can live and sleep.
'We've got a week's holiday in a caravan near the Lake District.'

car boot sale (noun) /kɑ: ˈbu:t seɪl/
an outdoor market where people sell items out the back of their car or on little tables next to their car.
'You can get some real bargains at a car boot sale.'

cardie (noun) /ˈkɑ:di/
a short form of 'cardigan', which is a sweater with buttons.
'I just bought a new cardie from H&M.'

carry coals to Newcastle (idiom)
to supply something to a place which already has a huge quantity of that thing and therefore doesn't need any more. It's a reference to the fact that Newcastle, and the surrounding areas in the northeast of England, used to have a big coal mining industry, so there was no need to carry any more coal there (also 'take coals to Newcastle').
'Trying to sell our semiconductor chips to Taiwanese car companies is like carrying coals to Newcastle.'

'carry the can'

carry the can (phrase)
to take responsibility or blame for something that went wrong.
'The government is going to have to carry the can for these high unemployment figures.'

cash machine/point (noun) /ˈkæʃ məʃiːn/
a machine that dispenses cash (also 'ATM').
'The only cash point in the village is a ten-minute walk away.'

catchment area (noun) /ˈkætʃmənt eəriə/
the geographical area that a state school draws its students from.
'We just moved into the catchment area for the top secondary school in Yorkshire.'

caught short (idiom)
to suddenly and unexpectedly need to go to the toilet, particularly when it's not convenient.
'Go to the loo before we leave. You don't want to get caught short on our hike.'

CBE (noun) /siː biː ˈiː/
CBE stands for Commander of the Order of the British Empire. It is a British honour given by the King for exceptional service and contributions to Britain.
'Benedict Cumberbatch has a CBE.'

ceilidh (noun) /ˈkeɪli/
a traditional event in Scotland, involving dancing and folk music.
'There's a ceilidh tonight at the town hall.'

cha (noun) /tʃɑː/ slang
a word for 'tea' that derives its origins from Chinese (also 'char').
'Does anyone fancy a cup of cha?'

champagne socialist (noun) /ʃæmˈpeɪn səʊʃəlɪst/
a derogatory term for someone who has socialist values while also living a wealthy lifestyle.
'Adam is a classic champagne socialist. He's always talking about inequality and yet he sends his kids to private school.'

Chancellor of the Exchequer (noun) /ˈtʃɑːnsələ əv ði ɪksˈtʃekə/
the person in the UK government who sets the annual budget and deals with other financial matters.
'The Chancellor of the Exchequer has kept taxes at the same rate for the last two years.'

TOM'S TIPS

The Eurostar takes just over two hours to go from London St Pancras, through the Channel Tunnel, to Paris. Perfect for a quick trip!

chancer (noun) /ˈtʃɑːnsə/
someone who is opportunistic and takes advantage of situations to benefit themselves. They may take risks and do things that other people wouldn't do.
'A lot of the guys I met in the banking industry were chancers.'

chance would be a fine thing (phrase)
used when you want something to happen, but there is almost no possibility of it actually happening.
A – 'Do you think England can win the World Cup this year?'
B – 'Chance would be a fine thing.'

(the) Channel Tunnel (noun) /ˈtʃænəl tʌnəl/
the train line running under the English Channel from England to France.
'I was just a little kid when the Queen opened the Channel Tunnel in 1994.'

chap (noun) /tʃæp/
a slightly old-fashioned word meaning 'boy' or 'man'.
'Right chaps, shall we head to the restaurant?'

charity shop (noun) /ˈtʃærɪti ʃɒp/
a shop that sells mostly second-hand items for the profit of a certain charity.
'As a way to practise their English, I always tell my students to volunteer in a charity shop.'

chat (someone) up (phrasal verb) /tʃæt ˈʌp/
to speak to someone in a manner that shows them you are sexually attracted to them.
'I've never had the courage to chat anyone up at a bar.'

(the) chattering classes (noun) /ˈtʃætərɪŋ klɑːsɪz/
a derogatory term for intellectual middle-class people who express their liberal views about politics and wider social issues.
'I wonder how popular this government is with the chattering classes.'

chav (noun) /tʃæv/ rude
a derogatory and offensive term for a young lower-class person.
'The stereotype of a chav is someone who wears a tracksuit and behaves in an anti-social way.'

chavvy (adjective) /ˈtʃævi/ rude
a derogatory and offensive word that describes something or someone that is seen as low-class and lacking education or taste.
'The shop I work in only sells cheap handbags and chavvy watches.'

cheeky (adjective) /ˈtʃiːki/
slightly rude but in a funny, playful way.
'At school, the teachers always said I was one of the cheekiest girls in the class.'

cheeky (adjective) /ˈtʃiːki/
used to describe doing something spontaneously that perhaps you know you shouldn't do, like have a drink or a cigarette.
'Do you fancy getting a cheeky pint before going home?'

'a cheeky pint'

cheerio (exclamation) /tʃɪəriˈəʊ/
a slightly old-fashioned way to say 'goodbye'.
'I'm going to head home now, cheerio!'

cheers (interjection) /tʃɪəz/
an informal way to say 'thank you'.
'Cheers for the lift, George. I really appreciate it.'

cheesed off (adjective) /tʃiːzd ˈɒf/ slang
annoyed.
'I'm really cheesed off Luca's not coming to my leaving do.'

Chelsea Pensioner (noun) /tʃelsi ˈpenʃənə/
a resident at the Royal Hospital Chelsea, a retirement home and nursing home in London for former members of the British Army. They are well known for wearing very distinctive red uniforms.
'You are quite likely to see a Chelsea Pensioner or two if you hang around the King's Road in west London.'

Chelsea tractor (noun) /tʃelsi ˈtræktə/
a derogatory and humorous term for a four-wheel-drive vehicle, typically driven around the streets of London. Chelsea is a particularly wealthy area of the city where they are said to be most commonly found.
'My school run is full of Chelsea tractors trying to drop their kids off.'

Chequers (noun) /ˈtʃekəz/
the name of the official country home of the British Prime Minister.
'The Prime Minister has been at Chequers all weekend, hosting the French President.'

chin chin (exclamation) /tʃɪn ˈtʃɪn/
an old-fashioned phrase used to express good wishes before drinking, similar to 'cheers'.
'Chin chin, everyone! Let's hope for a prosperous new year.'

chinwag (noun) /ˈtʃɪnwæg/
an informal conversation or chat.
A – 'Who was that on the phone?'
B – 'It was my Auntie Susie. She just wanted a quick chinwag.'

chippy (noun) /ˈtʃɪpi/
a fish-and-chip shop.
'Did you see there's a new chippy that's opened up on the seafront?'

choccy (noun) /ˈtʃɒki/
an informal term for 'chocolate'.
'Can you pick me up some choccy from the corner shop?'

chuffed (adjective) /tʃʌft/
an informal word meaning 'very pleased' (also 'chuffed to bits').
'You must be chuffed to bits with your job promotion.'

'I'm chuffed to bits'

chug (verb) /tʃʌg/ slang
to swallow a drink completely and without stopping.
'Come on guys, chug your drinks and let's go home.'

chugger (noun) /ˈtʃʌgə/ slang
someone that stands in the street trying to raise money for a specific charity. It's a portmanteau of 'charity' and 'mugger'.
'There is always a gang of chuggers standing outside the bank.'

chum (noun) /tʃʌm/
an old-fashioned word for 'friend'.
'I've got a few chums from my old school coming round for tea.'

chunder (verb) /ˈtʃʌndə/ slang
to vomit.
'Let me out of the car! I think I'm going to chunder.'

ciggy (noun) /ˈsɪgi/
short for 'cigarette' (also 'ciggie').
'I'm just going to pop out for a quick ciggy.'

civil servant (noun) /sɪvəl ˈsɜːvənt/
someone who works in the civil service.
'They are relocating a lot of civil servants to Manchester and Birmingham.'

civil service (noun) /sɪvəl ˈsɜːvɪs/
the permanent departments within a government and all the people that work for them. In the UK it is seen as politically impartial.
'Edward has worked for the civil service ever since leaving uni.'

clanger (noun) /ˈklæŋə/ slang
an embarrassing mistake.
'My boss dropped a real clanger in their presentation today.'

clapped out (adjective) /klæpt ˈaʊt/ slang
if a machine is clapped out, it has been used so much that it no longer works very well.
'It's impossible to do your job as a teacher when you've only got a clapped out photocopier to work with.'

claret (noun) /ˈklærət/ slang
a slang word for 'blood', which comes from the similarity of the colours of blood and claret wine.
'Did you see the fight outside the kebab shop last night? There was claret all over the pavement.'

clearing (noun) /ˈklɪərɪŋ/
the system British universities and colleges use to fill spare places on their courses. Anyone can apply who doesn't already have an offer from a university. Once A-level or Scottish Higher students receive their results in August, they can use clearing to find a place on a course they want.
'My A-level results weren't as good as I'd hoped for, so I used clearing to get a place at Cardiff Uni.'

clear-out (noun) /ˈkliə aʊt/
the act of sorting through all your things and throwing away what you don't need.
'I had a good clear-out at the weekend and gave loads of stuff to charity.'

clobber (noun) /ˈklɒbə/ slang
an informal word for clothes or personal items.
'I bought some new clobber with the money I got for Christmas.'

clock (verb) /klɒk/
to see or notice something.
'Did you clock Fernando trying to chat up Natsumi?'

coat (someone) off (phrasal verb) /kəʊt ˈɒf/ slang
to insult someone.
'I got completely coated off by my mates for getting a dragon tattoo.'

cobblers (noun) /ˈkɒbləz/ slang
an informal way of saying 'nonsense'.
A – 'I hardly ever use Instagram, honestly!'
B – 'Ha! What absolute cobblers! You're always on it.'

cock-a-hoop (adjective) /kɒk ə ˈhuːp/
a slightly old-fashioned word meaning happy and excited.
'Jess won the quiz and was cock-a-hoop for the rest of the evening.'

Cockney (noun) /ˈkɒkni/
someone from the East End of London. It's also the dialect and accent traditionally spoken by people from this area.
'Any self-respecting Cockney would know how to use rhyming slang.'

cock-up (noun) /ˈkɒk ʌp/ rude
a mistake.
'They've made a massive cock-up with our room booking. It looks like we'll have to find another hotel for the night.'

'codswallop'

codswallop (noun) /ˈkɒdzwɒləp/
an informal word for 'nonsense'.
A – 'I think Scotland will win the Six Nations this year.'
B – 'What absolute codswallop!'

C of E (noun) /siː əv ˈiː/
Church of England.
'I went to a C of E primary school.'

(the) collywobbles (noun) /ˈkɒliwɒbəlz/
a strong feeling of nervousness and mild fear.
'I always get the collywobbles before I fly.'

come a cropper (phrase)
used when an individual or team have suffered a defeat or got badly injured.
'Wales came a cropper against Italy.'

comprehensive school (noun) /kɒmprɪˈhensɪv skuːl/
a school for anyone in the UK between the ages of 11 and 18.
'My kids go to the local comprehensive down the road.'

Conservative Party (noun) /kənˈsɜːvətɪv pɑːti/
a British political party. Full name is the Conservative and Unionist Party.
'Margaret Thatcher was leader of the Conservative Party in the 1980s.'

constituency (noun) /kənˈstɪtʃuənsi/
an area in which someone is elected as its representative in parliament.
'The constituency of Hackney North has been a Labour stronghold for years.'

Cool Britannia (noun) /kuːl brɪˈtænjə/
a period during the 1990s in which there was an increased pride in British popular culture, led by the Spice Girls, Oasis, Blur, the election of Tony Blair, and New Labour.
'The years of Cool Britannia seem like a long time ago now.'

cop off (phrasal verb) /kɒp ˈɒf/ rude
a very informal phrase meaning to have a sexual encounter with someone.
'Did you see Ashley cop off with Maria at the Christmas Party?'

copper (noun) /ˈkɒpə/ slang
a police officer.
'I saw a pickpocket run along Oxford Street chased by two coppers.'

coppers (noun) /ˈkɒpəz/
an informal word for 1p and 2p coins.
'I've got nothing in my wallet except for a bunch of coppers.'

cor blimey! (interjection) /kɔː ˈblaɪmi/ slang
used to show surprise (often shortened to 'blimey!').
'Cor blimey! Have you seen what Emily wore to the wedding?'

corker (noun) /ˈkɔːkə/ slang
if something is a corker, it's particularly good.
'His best man speech was an absolute corker.'

'corner shop'

corner shop (noun) /ˈkɔːnə ʃɒp/
a local convenience store that sells basic food, drinks and everyday items.
'Dad's just popped to the corner shop to buy some milk and biscuits.'

Cornish pasty (noun) /ˈkɔːnɪʃ ˈpæsti/
a pastry filled with vegetables and meat, originating from Cornwall.
'When you go to Cornwall you have to try a Cornish pasty.'

Corrie (noun) /ˈkɒri/
an affectionate name for the popular soap opera 'Coronation Street'.
'If you grew up in the north of England, it was basically compulsory to watch Corrie.'

cottage pie (noun) /kɒtɪdʒ ˈpaɪ/
a dish of minced meat in gravy with a mashed potato topping that is cooked in the oven. Very similar to a shepherd's pie but made with beef, not lamb.
'My gran's cottage pie was award-winning.'

couldn't organise a piss-up in a brewery (idiom) rude
used to describe someone who is useless and unable to organise anything.
'This government couldn't organise a piss-up in a brewery.'

council estate (noun) /ˈkaʊnsəl ɪsteɪt/
an area of public housing provided by the government.
'My husband grew up on a council estate in Sheffield.'

council house/flat (noun) /ˈkaʊnsəl haʊs/
a house or flat provided by the local council for people on the lowest incomes.
'We've lived in a council flat in south Manchester for five years now.'

country bumpkin (noun) /ˈkʌntri ˈbʌmpkɪn/ rude
a derogatory term for someone from the countryside who is considered simple and unsophisticated.
'My Uncle Lloyd described himself as a bit of a country bumpkin. He hated visiting me in London.'

county (noun) /ˈkaʊnti/
an area used to subdivide the UK for administrative, geographical and political reasons, e.g. Dorset or Lancashire.
'The largest county in England is Yorkshire.'

crack on (phrase) slang
to start or continue to do something, often with enthusiasm and energy.
A – *'Do you mind if I start organising the stationery cupboard?'*
B – *'Not at all, crack on!'*

crack (someone) up (phrasal verb) /kræk ˈʌp/
to make someone laugh.
'No one cracks me up as much as my little nephew. He's hilarious!'

'crack on'

county council (noun) /kaʊnti ˈkaʊnsəl/
a group of elected people who represent a county.
'Kent County Council have worked very hard to improve the infrastructure in the local area.'

cozzie (noun) /ˈkɒzi/
an informal word for 'swimming costume' (also 'swimming cozzie').
'Don't forget to pack your cozzie for your holiday.'

cozzie livs (noun) /kɒzi ˈlɪvz/ slang
a shortened form of the 'cost of living crisis', which is the increased expense of everyday living costs like food and bills. It's a term that is most commonly used by younger English speakers.
'Sorry guys, I can't go on the trip this weekend. The cozzie livs is hitting me hard.'

crap (adjective) /kræp/ rude
an impolite way to say 'not very good'.
'Ugh I've had such a crap day at work.'

cream tea (noun) /kriːm ˈtiː/
a light meal taken in the afternoon consisting of tea, scones, clotted cream and jam. It originates in the West Country. However, there is a dispute as to how it should be eaten. In Cornwall, one is supposed to put the jam on first and the clotted cream on top, whereas in Devon it's clotted cream first then jam. It's a controversial issue! Either way, it's a British institution that should be tried by every visitor.
'I had one of the most divine cream teas while on holiday in St Ives.'

crease (someone) up (phrasal verb) /kriːs ˈʌp/
to make someone laugh.
'Arne's stories had us all creasing up.'

crikey! (exclamation) /ˈkraɪki/
used to show surprise.
'Crikey! Is that the time? I've got to shoot, I'm late for work.'

Crimbo (noun) /ˈkrɪmbəʊ/
a short form of 'Christmas' that's quite informal.
'Are you going to your parents house for Crimbo?'

crumbs! (exclamation) /krʌmz/
an old-fashioned way to express surprise or worry.
'Crumbs! I think we're going to miss our coach.'

Cup Final (noun) /ˈkʌp faɪnəl/
a term that traditionally referred to the FA Cup Final (football), but could be used to talk about any sporting cup final.
'The first cup final I remember was between Tottenham Hotspur and Nottingham Forest in 1991.'

cuppa (noun) /ˈkʌpə/
short for a cup of tea.
'I'm putting on the kettle. Who wants a cuppa?'

curate's egg (noun) /ˈkjʊərəts eg/
something that is partly good, but mostly bad.
'The new Ed Sheeran album is a bit of a curate's egg in my opinion.'

'curtain twitcher'

curtain twitcher (noun) /ˈkɜːtən twɪtʃə/
a disapproving term for someone who looks out of their window to see what all their neighbours are up to.
'It's very pretty around here, but it feels like the kind of place that would be full of curtain twitchers.'

cushty (adjective) /ˈkʊʃti/ slang
very good or pleasing.
'I have two weeks off work, so life is pretty cushty right now.'

cutlery (noun) /ˈkʌtləri/
the collective word for knives, forks and spoons.
'Can you put all those knives and forks in the cutlery drawer?'

CV (noun) /siː ˈviː/
short for 'curriculum vitae'. The document you submit to a potential employer with a list of your relevant education and work experience.
'You'll need to update your CV before applying for that job at Barclays.'

D

dab hand (noun) /dæb ˈhænd/
someone who has a high level of competency and skill in a certain activity.
'My dad is a dab hand at fixing electronics if you want him to take a look at your computer.'

daft (adjective) /dɑːft/
an informal word meaning 'foolish' or 'stupid'.
'Let's take the bus to the cinema. It'd be daft to try and walk there in this rain.'

damp squib (noun) /dæmp ˈskwɪb/
an event that doesn't live up to expectations and is ultimately disappointing.
'The after-party was a bit of a damp squib in the end.'

daylight robbery (idiom)
used to describe a situation where someone is charged an outrageously high price for something.
'This coffee and croissant cost nearly £7, it's daylight robbery!'

dead (adverb) /ded/ slang
very.
'That film was dead good, I want to watch it again.'

dear (adjective) /dɪə/
expensive.
'Blimey! Those shoes are a bit dear.'

dear (noun) /dɪə/
an affectionate term for someone.
'Hello dear, how can I help?'

death warmed up (phrase)
a humorous phrase meaning 'very ill'.
'Mate, go back to bed. You look like death warmed up.'

deffo (adverb) /ˈdefəʊ/ slang
short for 'definitely'.
A – 'Who do you think is going to win Traitors?'
B – 'Deffo Sarah! She's so cunning.'

detached house (noun) /dɪˈtætʃt ˈhaʊs/
a house that is not connected to any other houses.
'One day, I'd love to live in a detached house in the country.'

devvoed (adjective) /ˈdevəʊd/ slang
abbreviation of 'devastated' (mainly used in Liverpool).
'I'm proper devvoed Jessie can't come to our wedding.'

'dead good'

dickhead (noun) /ˈdɪkhed/ rude
a very rude insult for someone you think is an idiot.
'There was a dickhead on the bus wearing a Chelsea shirt and an Arsenal scarf.'

dicky (adjective) /ˈdɪki/ slang
used to refer to body parts to say that they are not well or working properly.
'My uncle isn't as active as he used to be because of his dicky heart.'

dicky bow (noun) /ˈdɪki bəʊ/
a bow tie.
'Are you wearing a dicky bow to the wedding?'

diddle (verb) /ˈdɪdəl/
to cheat or trick someone out of their money.
'The shop keeper tried to diddle me out of ten quid.'

diddums (interjection) /ˈdɪdəmz/
used to express sympathy to a child or sarcastically to an adult.
A – 'Daddy, I hurt my foot playing football.'
B – 'Awww, diddums!'

different gravy (phrase)
used to say that something or someone is so good you can't compare anything or anyone else to it.
'This Manchester City team are different gravy at the moment.'

dig (noun) /dɪg/
a comment that is deliberately meant to criticise or make fun of someone.
'Whenever I see my brother, he makes digs about how I'm not married yet.'

digs (noun) /dɪgz/ slang
an informal term for a place of residence.
'My student digs were located miles from campus and weren't very luxurious.'

dim (adjective) /dɪm/
not very intelligent.
'Harry is a sweet little boy, but he can be a little dim sometimes.'

din-dins (noun) /ˈdɪndɪnz/
a childlike way to say 'dinner'.
'What's for din-dins, Dad?'

ding dong (noun) /ˈdɪŋ dɒŋ/ slang
an informal term for a very lively argument.
'My ex-boyfriend and I used to have massive ding dongs while travelling.'

dinky (adjective) /ˈdɪŋki/
small in a positive way.
'Awww, your baby is gorgeous. Look at how dinky her hands are!'

dinnae (contraction) /ˈdɪni/
a Scottish form of 'do not'.
'Dinnae be late for dinner tonight!'

dirty weekend (noun) /dɜːti wiːˈkend/
slang
a weekend away with a sexual partner with the focus on having lots of sex.
'Javi and I have booked a dirty weekend in Paris next month.'

dishy (adjective) /ˈdɪʃi/
an old-fashioned term for 'good-looking'. Usually used to refer to men.
'My mum always thought Cliff Richard was very dishy.'

divvy (noun) /ˈdɪvi/ rude
an informal word for 'idiot' (also 'div').
'Charlie, why are you acting like such a divvy?'

divvy up (phrasal verb) /dɪvi ˈʌp/
to share or divide something.
'If we win the lottery, we will have to divvy up the winnings between us.'

DIY (abbreviation) /diː aɪ ˈwaɪ/
DIY is short for 'do-it-yourself'. This is the activity of making or repairing something inside your home instead of paying someone else to do it.
'I'm doing some DIY this morning and then I'm off to the gym this afternoon.'

do (noun) /duː/ slang
a party.
'Are you coming to Chinami's leaving do?'

do (verb) /duː/ slang
to punish or prosecute someone.
'I've been done twice for speeding by the police.'

do (verb) /duː/ slang
to rip off, outsmart, or cheat someone. Often used in the passive.
A – 'How much was that jacket?'
B – '£120.'
A – 'You've been done, mate!'

do a runner (phrase) slang
to leave somewhere like a restaurant without paying.
'We used to do a runner from cafes all the time as teenagers.'

dob (someone) in (phrasal verb) /dɒb ˈɪn/ slang
to inform a person of authority about someone's illegal actions or wrongdoings.
'I'm going to dob you in to the teacher unless you give me back my pencil case.'

doddle (noun) /ˈdɒdəl/
something really easy to do.
'My Spanish test was an absolute doddle.'

dodgy (adjective) /ˈdɒdʒi/ slang
dangerous.
'I wouldn't walk around here at night time. It can be a bit dodgy.'

dodgy (adjective) /ˈdɒdʒi/ slang
untrustworthy.
'I'm looking to move flats because my landlord is super dodgy.'

doer-upper (noun) /duːə ˈʌpə/
a house not in good condition that someone buys in order to make improvements and increase its value.
'My sister and her husband have bought a bit of a doer-upper in Leeds.'

dogsbody (noun) /ˈdɒgzbɒdi/
a person who is asked to do all the menial tasks and jobs no one else wants to do.
'The worst job I ever had was at a garden centre where I was basically just a dogsbody.'

(the) dog's bollocks (phrase) rude
a rude way to say 'brilliant' or 'fantastic' (synonym of 'mutt's nuts').
'Elif is the dog's bollocks when it comes to darts. She's unbeatable.'

dog's dinner (phrase)
an informal phrase for something that's messy, disorganised or badly done.
'I made a dog's dinner of my final essay – I'm definitely going to fail the course!'

do (someone's) head in (phrase)
an informal phrase to say someone is really annoying you (also 'do (someone's) nut in').
'The kids have been doing my head in all day. I can't wait for the school holidays to end.'

(anything/nothing/something) doing (phrase)
an informal phrase meaning 'things happening'.
'I went to Steve's house party to see what was going on, but there wasn't anything doing so I came home.'

(the) dole (noun) /dəʊl/
an informal term for the money the government gives people who are unemployed. It is also known as the Jobseeker's Allowance.
'My sister-in-law has been on the dole since she lost her job last year.'

donkey's years (noun) /ˈdɒŋkiz jɪəz/ slang
an informal way of saying 'a long time'.
'I haven't seen my school friends for donkey's years.'

do one! (exclamation) /ˈduː wʌn/ rude
a rude informal way to tell someone to go away.
A – 'There's no way you are passing your driving test tomorrow!'
B – 'Do one!'

do (someone) over (phrasal verb) /duː ˈəʊvə/ slang
to attack someone with punches and kicks.
'He was done over by a group of lads while walking home last night.'

dosh (noun) /dɒʃ/ slang
money.
'How much dosh have you got on you?'

doss (noun) /dɒs/ slang
if something is a doss, it is very easy and doesn't require a lot of effort.
'To be honest, I don't really like my job, but it's a bit of a doss.'

doss around/about (phrasal verb) /dɒs əˈraʊnd/ slang
to spend your time not doing very much.
'Isn't it time you got a job, Chris? You've been dossing around for weeks.'

dosshouse (noun) /ˈdɒshaʊs/ slang
a place where homeless people can spend the night.
'When I was evicted from my old flat, I had to spend a few nights in a dosshouse.'

dotty (adjective) /ˈdɒti/
an informal way to say someone or someone's behaviour is slightly mad or eccentric.
'My aunt is a bit dotty – she wears a hat all year round and talks to her plants.'

double-barrelled name (noun) /dʌbəl bærəld ˈneɪm/
a family name made up of two surnames put together, usually joined by a hyphen, e.g. Walker-Peters.
'It's become more and more common to have a double-barrelled name these days.'

double dutch (noun) /dʌbəl ˈdʌtʃ/
spoken or written English that is incomprehensible.
'Have you read the CEO's email to the board? It's double dutch!'

'double dutch'

'duck and dive'

double yellow line (noun) /dʌbəl jeləʊ ˈlaɪn/
the two yellow lines painted along the sides of some streets. It indicates that you may not park your car there.
'You can't park on St James' Lane, it's got a double yellow line!'

dough (noun) /dəʊ/ slang
money.
'Can you lend me some dough until payday?'

down under (phrase) /daʊn ˈʌndə/
an informal way to refer to Australia or New Zealand.
'He's been living down under with his boyfriend for five years.'

dram (noun) /dræm/
a Scottish term for a small amount of whisky.
'Would you like a wee dram before bed?'

draw (noun) /drɔː/
the result of a game where both opponents end with the same score.
A – 'Who won the game last night?'
B – 'It was a draw.'

draw (verb) /drɔː/
to end a game with the same number of points as the opponent.
'I think Liverpool's going to draw with Everton in tonight's game.'

dreich (adjective) /driːx/
a Scottish word which is used to describe weather as gloomy and bleak.
A – 'How's the weather up there in the Highlands today?'
B – 'Absolutely dreich!'

drink-driving (noun) /drɪŋk ˈdraɪvɪŋ/
the act of driving under the influence of alcohol.
'The police pulled him over under the suspicion of drink-driving.'

dross (noun) /drɒs/
something that is poor quality or of no use.
'To be honest, most of the programmes on TV these days are absolute dross.'

dual carriageway (noun) /djuːəl ˈkærɪdʒweɪ/
a road with two lanes going in each direction that is divided by a strip of grass and usually a barrier.
'This dual carriageway takes us all the way to Blackpool.'

duck (noun) /dʌk/
an affectionate term used particularly in the north of England (also 'ducky').
'How are you, duck? Were you out last night?'

duck and dive (idiom)
to use your resourcefulness and cunning to deal with a problem, situation or possibly an illegal activity.
'Where I grew up you had to do a bit of ducking and diving to survive.'

dutch courage (noun) /dʌtʃ ˈkʌrɪdʒ/
the confidence someone gets from drinking alcohol.
'If I'm going to make a speech at my sister's wedding, I'm going to need a little dutch courage.'

E

earbashing (noun) /ˈɪəbæʃɪŋ/ slang
angry criticism said to someone.
'My boss gave me an earbashing for sending out the report without her checking it first.'

early doors (adverb) /ɜːli ˈdɔːz/
at an early point or near to the beginning.
'I told my boss early doors that I wouldn't be able to work over the Christmas holidays.'

East Ender (noun) /iːst ˈendə/
someone from the East End of London.
'My grandad is a proper East Ender. He lived all his life in and around Bethnal Green.'

easy peasy (lemon squeezy) (phrase)
a playful or childlike way to say something is easy. It's common to shorten the phrase to just 'easy peasy'.
'That driving test was easy peasy.'

eff and blind/jeff (phrase)
if you eff and blind or eff and jeff, you use swear words.
'I'm furious with Patricio! He was effing and blinding around the kids.'

effing (adjective) /ˈefɪŋ/ rude
used to add emphasis and avoid using the word 'fuck'.
'There's no effing way I'm going to their wedding after the way they treated me!'

eff off (exclamation) /ˈef ɒf/ rude
used to tell someone to go away. It's considered rude, but less rude than actually saying 'fuck off'. It's commonly used to report back a conversation in a more polite manner than it originally took place.
'The shopkeeper refused to serve the man and told him to eff off.'

TOM'S TIPS

One of Britain's favourite soap operas is 'EastEnders'. It is set in a fictional part of east London called Walford. This is a portmanteau of two real areas in east London – Walthamstow and Stratford.

TOM'S TIPS

The EPL was founded in 1992, and Manchester United have won it a record 13 times. One of the greatest sporting shocks of all time came in the 2015/16 season, when the title was won by Leicester City.

egg-chasing (noun) /ˈeg tʃeɪsɪŋ/ slang
a humorous and dismissive term for 'rugby'.
'I'm more of a football girl – I don't like all this egg-chasing nonsense.'

elevenses (noun) /ɪˈlevənzɪz/
a break in the late morning in which one might have a coffee or light snack. It's usually around 11 o'clock, hence the name elevenses.
'I brought in some biscuits for our elevenses.'

Estuary English (noun) /ˈestjʊəri ɪŋglɪʃ/
an accent that is found in the southeast of England around London. It's a mix of Received Pronunciation and Cockney.
'You hear a lot of Estuary English where I live in Kent.'

eurosceptic (noun) /jʊərəʊˈskeptɪk/
someone who opposes Britain's involvement with the European Union.
'It feels like you are less of a eurosceptic than you used to be, Dan. Is that fair to say?'

'eurosceptic'

EPL (noun) /iː piː ˈel/
an acronym for the English Premier League.
'Millions of people around the world watch the EPL.'

ex-council (adjective) /eks ˈkaʊnsəl/
refers to a flat or house that used to belong to the local council and was used for public housing but has since been bought by the tenant and is therefore privately owned.
'All the properties the estate agent showed us were ex-council.'

F

FA (noun) /ef ˈeɪ/
an abbreviation for 'Football Association'. This is the governing body that runs football in England.
'The FA was founded in 1863.'

FA Cup (noun) /ef eɪ ˈkʌp/
first played in 1871, the FA Cup is the oldest national football competition in the world. All teams who belong to England's Football Association compete to win the silver trophy in May every year.
'Who do you think is going to win the FA Cup this season?'

fag (noun) /fæg/ slang
a cigarette.
'My grandma smokes 30 fags a day.'

fair do's (phrase)
an informal way to accept what someone has said, similar to 'fair enough'.
A – 'I much prefer the British version of The Office to the American one.'
B – 'Fair do's.'

faith school (noun) /ˈfeɪθ skuːl/
a school in the United Kingdom that teaches a general curriculum, but which also has a formal link to a specific religion or faith-based organisation.
'I'd like my children to go to a faith school if possible.'

fancy (verb) /ˈfænsi/
to be attracted to someone sexually.
'All the girls used to fancy this boy called John Williams at my school.'

fancy (verb) /ˈfænsi/
to want or desire something.
'I really fancy getting a Chinese takeaway tonight. What do you reckon?'

fancy dress (noun) /fænsi ˈdres/
the special clothes people wear to themed parties.
'I've told everyone to come to my birthday party in fancy dress.'

fanny (noun) /ˈfæni/ rude
a vulgar word for a woman's genitals. It's also used as an offensive word for 'idiot'.
'Fanny is one of my least-favourite words to talk about female genitalia.'

fanny around (phrasal verb) /fæni əˈraʊnd/ rude
to waste time instead of getting on with the task you need to get done (also 'fanny about').
'Stop fannying around and fill in the application form.'

Father Christmas (noun) /fɑːðə ˈkrɪsməs/
a man in a red suit who brings presents to children around the world on 24th/25th December (also 'Santa Claus').
'Father Christmas was very generous this year and brought me and my little brother new bikes!'

fell (noun) /fel/
an Old Norse word for 'hill', used mostly in the north of England.
'There's a group of fell-runners in my town and they've asked if I want to join.'

festive season (noun) /ˈfestɪv siːzən/
a period of time starting before Christmas and continuing through to New Year's Eve.
'Are you going back up north for the festive season?'

flash (adjective) /ˈflæʃ/
used to describe someone or something ostentatious, often in a disapproving way (also 'flashy').
'I'm not into flash cars and expensive watches.'

'fill your boots'

fill your boots (phrase)
an informal phrase used to mean 'have as much as you want', e.g. at a buffet or at dinner.
'We've laid on a few snacks and drinks for you guys, so please fill your boots.'

fit (adjective) /fɪt/ slang
a slang word to describe someone as attractive or hot.
'Have you got any fit friends you can set me up on a date with?'

fitba (noun) /ˈfɪtbɑː/
a word that denotes the Scottish pronunciation of 'football'.
'Did you go to the fitba on Saturday?'

fiver (noun) /ˈfaɪvə/
an informal word for five pounds.
A – 'How much are those flowers?'
B – 'They're a fiver.'

flag (verb) /flæg/
to get tired or weak.
'Can we stop walking for a minute guys? I'm flagging a little.'

flaming (adjective) /ˈfleɪmɪŋ/ slang
used to intensify something particularly in an angry way.
'You flaming idiot! You nearly broke my foot with that dumbbell.'

(the) flicks (noun) /flɪks/
an old-fashioned term for the cinema.
'Shall we go to the flicks on Friday night?'

flies (noun) /flaɪz/
the zipper on a pair of trousers (also 'fly').
'Mate, your flies are undone, again!'

flog (verb) /flɒg/ slang
to sell something, usually quickly, and for a reduced price.
'Our neighbours are trying to flog their old Ford Escort.'

fluff (verb) /flʌf/
to fail to do something successfully.
'I hope I don't fluff my lines in the play tonight.'

fluke (noun) /fluːk/
something good that comes from luck or chance.
'It was a pure fluke that I got this job.'

flukey (adjective) /ˈfluːki/
benefiting from luck or chance.
'Manchester United scored one of the flukiest goals you will ever see.'

flutter (noun) /ˈflʌtə/
a small bet.
'I always like to have a flutter on the Grand National.'

fly-tipping (noun) /ˈflaɪ tɪpɪŋ/
the illegal dumping of unwanted things, like sofas or kitchen appliances. They are usually left next to roads and other public locations.
'Fly-tipping has become a real problem around here since the police stopped patrolling the streets.'

footy (noun) /ˈfʊti/
a shortened term for 'football'.
'Are you going to come round to watch the footy tonight?'

Foreign Office (noun) /ˈfɒrɪn ɒfɪs/
the British government department that is concerned with issues in other countries.
'There was a fabulous documentary about the Foreign Office on the BBC.'

fortnight (noun) /ˈfɔːtnaɪt/
two weeks.
'The cleaner comes once a fortnight.'

free school (noun) /ˈfriː skuːl/
a school in England that is free to attend as well as being non-profit making, state-funded and independent of the local authority.
'Once I get my PGCE I'm going to apply for a job at a free school near me.'

fresher (noun) /ˈfreʃə/
a first-year university student.
'The town is starting to feel busier; I guess it's because all the freshers are arriving and moving into their halls of residence.'

freshers' week (noun) /ˈfreʃəz wiːk/
the first week of university for new students, in which social events are organised.
'I remember the Arctic Monkeys played at my freshers' week ball.'

fringe (noun) /ˈfrɪndʒ/
a hairstyle in which the front of the hair hangs over the forehead, but stops above the eyes.
'My parents insisted I have a fringe up until the age of 13.'

front bench (noun) /frʌnt ˈbentʃ/
the place in the House of Commons where senior ministers of the government and the opposition party sit, or the ministers that sit there.
'The Prime Minister is confident his front bench will support his new plans.'

front bencher (noun) /frʌnt ˈbentʃə/
a government minister or member of the shadow cabinet.
'Government front benchers are furious about the Prime Minster's decision to enter into discussions with the opposition leader.'

'Freshers' week has become a huge thing in the UK, with each university putting on a whole range of events for new students. There are "get-to-know-you" activities, taster sessions, club nights and parties going on throughout the week. It's an excellent opportunity to make new friends and settle in to uni life.'

Teacher Tom

fry-up (noun) /ˈfraɪ ʌp/
another phrase for a full English breakfast.
'My grandad used to have a fry-up every morning before work!'

fuck (exclamation) /fʌk/ rude
an extremely rude word used to show anger.
'Fuck! We've missed the last bus!'

fuck (noun) /fʌk/ rude
a very rude way to add emphasis to a statement.
'Where the fuck are my shoes?'

fuck (verb) /fʌk/ rude
an extremely rude way to say to have sexual intercourse.
'Did you guys fuck?'

fuck all (phrase) rude
a very rude term meaning nothing at all (see also sweet FA).
'The airline have done fuck all to help me find my lost luggage.'

fuck off! (exclamation) /ˈfʌk ɒf/ rude
used to show a strong feeling of contempt or anger.
A – 'Did you see they've cancelled our flight?'
B – 'Fuck off! Are you being serious?'

fuck off (phrasal verb) /ˈfʌk ɒf/ rude
an extremely rude way to tell someone to go away.
'Can you fuck off so I can read my book in peace?'

fuck-off (adjective) /ˈfʌk ɒf/ rude
very large or impressive.
'They've bought a big fuck-off house in Surrey worth over 2 million quid.'

fuck (someone) off (phrasal verb) /fʌk ˈɒf/ rude
to really annoy someone.
'Oh my goodness, my laptop is really fucking me off today! Why does it keep on crashing?'

full English breakfast (noun) /fʊl ɪŋglɪʃ ˈbrekfəst/
a traditional English breakfast usually consisting of sausages, eggs, bacon, baked beans and other items, such as tomatoes, mushrooms, black pudding and toast. Regional cousins include the full Scottish breakfast, the Ulster Fry and the full Welsh breakfast, each with its own local twist.
'When you visit England, you've got to try a full English breakfast.'

full monty (noun) /fʊl ˈmɒnti/
used to describe something that has everything you require or expect. It is also a term used for a male striptease (see the film 'The Full Monty' for more details).
'Our safari was amazing. We saw lions, tigers, elephants, gorillas – the full monty!'

full of beans (phrase)
having a lot of energy and enthusiasm.
A – 'Good morning, how are you feeling?'
B – 'I'm full of beans today!'

further education (noun) /fɜːðə edjʊˈkeɪʃən/
education for people who have left school but who are not at university.
'It's important for more people to have access to further education.'

(the) fuzz (noun) /fʌz/ slang
the police.
'It took ten minutes for the fuzz to finally arrive and break up the fighting.'

G

gadgie (noun) /ˈgædʒiː/ slang
a slang word for 'man', used in eastern Scotland and northeast England (also 'gadge').
'There's a gadgie at work who used to play rugby for Scotland under-21s.'

gaff (noun) /gæf/ slang
a house.
'We're about to drive past Luke and Luisa's new gaff.'

gaffe (noun) /gæf/
a mistake.
'Ross made a terrible gaffe at his wedding when he said Rachel's name and not Emily's.'

'gaffer'

gaffer (noun) /ˈgæfə/ slang
the boss.
'Have you asked the gaffer if you can have Friday off?'

gag (noun) /gæg/
an informal word for 'joke'.
'Have you heard Michael McIntyre's gag about American English words?'

gagging (for something) (verb) /ˈgægɪŋ/ slang
to be desperate for something.
'I'm absolutely gagging for a glass of water.'

gagging for it (phrase) rude
a rude phrase to suggest someone is eager for sex.
'Go and chat to that guy over there, he's clearly gagging for it.'

gallus (adjective) /ˈgæləs/
a Scottish word describing someone who is daring or bold.
'Isla's a gallus girl for climbing Ben Nevis on her own.'

gammon (noun) /ˈgæmən/ slang
an insult for a red-faced angry old man with right-wing views. It was coined by a writer who used the term to describe a group of men who supported Brexit and supposedly had faces that resembled gammon steaks.
'The town I live in is absolutely full of gammon.'

gammy (adjective) /ˈgæmi/ slang
if a part of your body is gammy, it is painful, stiff or causes you difficulty.
'I've had a gammy knee ever since I did the marathon.'

gan (verb) /gæn/ slang
slang for 'go', used in northeast England.
'I'm gannin' down the chippy, do you want anything?'

gander (noun) /ˈgændə/
a look around or at something.
'Let's have a gander around the old town and see if we can find a nice place to eat.'

'gap year'

gap year (noun) /ˈɡæp jɪə/
a year between leaving school and starting university in which the individual usually works or travels to gain some life experience.
'He spent his gap year working on a vineyard in Tuscany.'

gastropub (noun) /ˈɡæstrəʊpʌb/
a pub that serves high-quality food.
'They are turning the old cinema into a huge gastropub.'

gawp (verb) /ɡɔːp/
to look at someone or something for a long time in a rude or stupid way.
'Mina, stop gawping at the barista and go chat to him.'

gazump (verb) /ɡəˈzʌmp/
if you are buying a house and the seller agrees to sell it to you, but then sells it to someone else for more money, you have been gazumped.
'We thought we'd bought a semi-detached house in York, but frustratingly we were gazumped at the last minute.'

GBH (noun) /dʒiː biː ˈeɪtʃ/
abbreviation for 'grievous bodily harm'. This is a legal term for a physical attack by one person on another.
'He's in court for GBH and armed robbery.'

GCSE (noun) /dʒiː siː es ˈiː/
General Certificate of Secondary Education. A qualification in a certain subject taken by students in the UK (except Scotland) between the ages of 14 and 16. Once students complete their GCSEs they can go on to study A-levels.
'I took nine GCSEs and managed to get all sevens.'

geet walla (adjective) /ɡiːt ˈwɒlə/ slang
a slang term meaning 'very big' that's used in Newcastle.
'There was a geet walla queue at the bus stop so I decided to walk.'

geezer (noun) /ˈɡiːzə/ slang
a slang word for a man. It's often used with specific collocations, e.g. top geezer, diamond geezer, old geezer and dodgy geezer.
'I got chatting to this old geezer in the pub who said he knew Bobby Moore, the England captain at the 1966 World Cup.'

gentry (noun) /ˈdʒentri/
the aristocratic class who own land around Britain.
'The House of Lords used to be made up of aristocrats and landed gentry.'

(the) gents (noun) /dʒents/
a polite term for 'male toilets'.
'The gents are upstairs and along the corridor.'

Geordie (noun) /ˈdʒɔːdi/
someone from Newcastle.
'My flatmate is a Geordie and she pops back home to Newcastle every other weekend.'

get a wriggle on (phrase)
used to mean 'hurry up'.
'Come on kids, get a wriggle on otherwise we'll be late for Grandad's birthday.'

get (one's) end away (phrase) rude
if someone gets their end away, they have sex.
'On Friday nights all Teddy cares about is getting his end away.'

get (one's) head down (phrase)
if someone gets their head down, they work hard and focus on what they're doing.
'Tomorrow, I'm going to get my head down and revise for my French exam.'

get (one's) kit off (phrase) slang
a humorous phrase meaning to remove your clothes.
'Come on lads, get your kit off!'

get off with (phrase) slang
to have a romantic kiss and cuddle with someone (similar to 'make out' with someone).
'All I remember from my school discos was teenagers getting off with each other and bad music.'

get on someone's wick/nerves/tits (phrase) rude
if you get on someone's wick/nerves/tits, you're annoying them. While using 'wick' and 'nerves' in the phrase are perfectly acceptable, the use of 'tits' is considered quite rude.
'I love my brother but he's really starting to get on my tits.'

get stuck in (phrase)
to do something in a determined and enthusiastic way.
'Come on, let's get stuck into the cleaning so we can relax tonight.'

get the hump (with someone) (phrase)
if you get the hump with someone, you're upset or angry with them.
'Why have you got the hump with me? Did I do something wrong?'

get the nod (phrase)
to be selected or given permission.
'Two Celtic youngsters have got the nod from the manager for Saturday's match with Rangers.'

get your knickers in a twist (idiom)
a humorous phrase meaning to get upset or annoyed about something.
'Jakub, don't get your knickers in a twist. We'll get to the airport on time!'

ghastly (adjective) /ˈgɑːstli/
very bad or unpleasant.
A – 'How was your weekend in Wales?'
B – 'It was wonderful although the weather was ghastly for most of the time.'

ginnel/gennel (noun) /ˈgɪnəl/ or /ˈgenəl/
a narrow alleyway between houses in the north of England.
'We used to play games in the ginnels by my gran's house in Blackburn.'

gip (verb) /gɪp/ slang
to retch or feel like vomiting
'The strong smell of fish in that market made me gip.'

git (noun) /gɪt/
an unpleasant individual.
'I don't talk to my neighbour. He's a bit of a git if I'm honest.'

'get stuck in'

'I'll give you a bell'

give (someone) a bell/buzz/ring/call (phrase)
an informal phrase meaning to call someone on the phone.
'I'll give you a bell when I get out of class.'

give over! (phrase)
a way to tell someone to stop doing something that's annoying.
A – 'Are you going to finally ask Chiara out?'
B – 'Oh give over! You know I'm not interested.'

give (someone) stick (phrase)
to criticise or verbally abuse someone. It can also mean to tease someone in a joking way.
'The fans gave the opposing players a lot of stick when they came onto the football pitch.'

giz (verb) /gɪz/ slang
a slang variation of 'give us'.
'Giz back my pen, you little thief!'

Glasgow kiss (noun) /glɑːzgəʊ ˈkɪs/
a euphemism for a headbutt, i.e. using your head to hit someone.
'She's threatened to give me a Glasgow kiss if I don't leave the party now.'

Glastonbury (noun) /ˈglæstənbərɪ/
Britain's biggest contemporary music and arts festival, located in the southwest of England (shortened to 'Glasto').
'Do you know who is headlining Glastonbury this year?'

Glaswegian (noun) /glæzˈwiːdʒən/
someone from Glasgow.
'I have always found Glaswegians to be incredibly welcoming and friendly.'

GMT (noun) /dʒiː em ˈtiː/
the abbreviation for 'Greenwich Mean Time', which is the time measured from the Royal Observatory in Greenwich, London.
'We are going live on YouTube at 3 p.m. GMT.'

gob (noun) /gɒb/ slang
your mouth.
'Shut your gob!'

gobby (adjective) /ˈgɒbi/ slang
talking in a loud, opinionated way.
'Their son has turned into a right gobby so-and-so.'

go belly up (idiom)
if a company goes belly up, it fails and goes bankrupt.
'My uncle's business went belly up during the recession in 2008.'

gobsmacked (adjective) /ˈgɒbsmækt/
very surprised.
'When I found out I'd got a place at Oxford I was completely gobsmacked.'

go down (phrasal verb) /gəʊ ˈdaʊn/ slang
to be sent to prison.
'Gemma's boyfriend went down for armed robbery.'

go down (phrasal verb) /gəʊ ˈdaʊn/
when a team moves to a lower division at the end of a season because of bad results.
'It hard to say which three teams are going down this season.'

go off (phrasal verb) /gəʊ ˈɒf/
if food goes off, it turns bad, changes smell or colour, and becomes inedible.
'I'm going to get some more eggs – these ones have gone off.'

go off on one (phrase) slang
to suddenly start getting angry and shouting or ranting about something.
'Last night my dad suddenly started going off on one about how social media is ruining society.'

go spare (phrase) slang
to become very angry.
'Our teacher went spare when he realised the whole class had cheated in the test.'

go tits-up (idiom) rude
if something goes tits-up, it goes wrong or fails. It's a very informal phrase and considered slightly rude.
'My plans to throw Helen a surprise birthday party have gone completely tits-up. She saw a text I sent a friend with all the details.'

(the) gods (noun) /gɒdz/
an informal term for the seats in a theatre that are furthest from the stage and highest up.
'Even though we were sat in the gods, we could see the play perfectly well.'

golly gosh! (exclamation) /ˈgɒli gɒʃ/
an old-fashioned way to show surprise or worry.
'Golly gosh! I never knew my neighbour was the daughter of a famous film star.'

goose pimples (noun) /ˈguːs pɪmpəlz/
tiny raised areas of your skin that occur because you are excited, nervous or thrilled in some way.
'Watching my sister walk down the aisle gave me goose pimples.'

Gordon Bennett! (exclamation) /ˈgɔːdən ˈbenɪt/
an old-fashioned phrase used to show surprise or annoyance.
'Gordon Bennett! Have you seen what the kids have done to the kitchen?'

gormless (adjective) /ˈgɔːmləs/
foolish or slow-witted.
A – 'Is that you in the photo? You look so young!'
B – 'Yeah, that's me and my friends at school. Wow! We look so gormless'.

'Each city has a term for the people that are from there. The technical term is a "demonym". People from Newcastle are "Geordies", someone from Manchester is a "Mancunian" and if you come from Liverpool, you are a "Liverpudlian" or a "Scouser". See if you can find any more in the book.'

Teacher Tom

GP (noun) /dʒiː ˈpiː/
a general practitioner, i.e. a doctor who deals with general medical issues in a local clinic and not a hospital.
'I've got to see my GP about vaccinations for my trip to Thailand.'

graft (verb) /grɑːft/
to work hard.
'You have to really graft if you want to be successful in this world.'

grafter (noun) /ˈgrɑːftə/
an informal term for someone who works hard.
'I'm so impressed with the builders doing up my house, they are such grafters.'

grammar school (noun) /ˈgræmə skuːl/
a type of state school in Britain for children aged 11–18. All students are required to pass an entrance exam. They are much less common now than in the past.
'My grandmother was the first in our family to go to a grammar school.'

grand (adjective) /grænd/
great or enjoyable.
'We had a grand time in Belfast last weekend. I really recommend going.'

grand (noun) /grænd/ slang
one thousand pounds sterling.
'Did you hear the CEO is getting a fifty-grand bonus?'

(the) Grand National (noun) /grænd ˈnæʃənəl/
the nation's biggest horse race, held at Aintree racecourse near Liverpool.
'This year the Grand National will be run on 9th April.'

grass (noun) /grɑːs/ slang
someone who tells the police or an authority figure information about another person's wrongdoing (usually criminal).
'The gang never found out who the grass was.'

grass on (someone) (phrasal verb) /ˈgrɑːs ɒn/ slang
if you grass on someone, you tell the police or authorities about their wrongdoing (also 'grass (someone) up').
'Simon grassed on me to the teacher about copying his homework.'

greasy spoon (noun) /griːsi ˈspuːn/ slang
a cheap and cheerful restaurant that sells simple home-cooked food, like full English breakfasts, chips, burgers, etc. (also 'caff').
'My grandad used to take me to the local greasy spoon every Saturday for breakfast.'

greedy guts (noun) /ˈgriːdi gʌts/
someone who is greedy, especially about food.
'Did you eat all the chocolate biscuits? You are such a greedy guts!'

‘let’s pick up some grub’

green belt (noun) /ˈgriːn belt/
the area of protected countryside surrounding towns and cities in which there are restrictions on building development.
‘It’s so important we protect the green belt.’

grockle (noun) /ˈgrɒkəl/ rude
a derogatory term used in Devon and Cornwall for a holidaymaker or tourist (also ‘grock’).
‘The town is full of grocks during summer – it’s unbearable.’

grotty (adjective) /ˈgrɒti/
dirty or unpleasant.
‘I’ve stayed in some grotty hotels in my time, but this one was the worst.’

ground floor (noun) /graʊnd ˈflɔː/
the floor that is at the same level as the ground or street.
‘My gran’s bought a flat on the ground floor because her mobility’s not so good any more.’

grub (noun) /grʌb/ slang
food.
‘Let’s pick up some grub on the way home.’

gutted (adjective) /ˈgʌtɪd/ slang
very disappointed.
‘Oh look, the kids are gutted about the match. Maybe we should do something to cheer them up.’

(the) gutter press (noun) /gʌtə ˈpres/
sensationalist or low-quality newspapers.
‘As a journalist, Tony only ever worked for the gutter press.’

guv’nor (noun) /ˈgʌvnə/ slang
a slang term for ‘governor’, but also used more generally as a greeting to show respect to someone in authority.
‘Alright guv’nor, how’s it going?’

Guy Fawkes Night (noun) /gaɪ ˈfɔːks naɪt/
a celebration on 5th November when British people light bonfires and fireworks to remember Guy Fawkes and the Gunpowder Plot to blow up the Houses of Parliament in 1605.
‘There’s a huge fireworks display at Alexandra Palace on Guy Fawkes Night.’

gyp (noun) /dʒɪp/ slang
pain, discomfort or trouble.
‘My ankle is really giving me gyp.’

H

hacked off (adjective) /hækt ˈɒf/
an informal way to say 'annoyed'.
'I am so hacked off I didn't get invited to Marlon and Emily's wedding.'

hackney carriage/cab (noun) /ˈhækni ˈkærɪdʒ/
the proper term for a London black taxi.
'There's nothing more iconic in London than the hackney carriage.'

Hadrian's Wall (noun) /ˈheɪdrɪənz wɔːl/
a wall across the north of England between England and Scotland, which was built to keep the northern tribes out of Roman Britain.
'I'd love to do the walk all the way along Hadrian's wall.'

haggis (noun) /ˈhægɪs/
a traditional Scottish dish made of a sheep's or calf's offal mixed with suet, oatmeal and seasoning.
'If you go to Scotland, you have to try haggis.'

half (noun) /hɑːf/
half a pint (284 ml).
A – 'Do you want a pint of lager?'
B – 'Just a half for me, thanks.'

half-arsed (adjective) /hɑːf ˈɑːst/ rude
careless and lazy.
'She made a half-arsed attempt to apologise after forgetting my birthday.'

half-board (noun) /hɑːf ˈbɔːd/
a hotel room which also includes breakfast and either lunch or dinner.
'We've booked two nights half-board in a seaside hotel in Norfolk.'

half term (noun) /hɑːf ˈtɜːm/
a week-long break for schools in the middle of each term.
'Are you guys going away for half term?'

halls of residence (noun) /hɔːlz əv ˈrezɪdəns/
a residential building where students live (also 'halls').
'Which halls are you living in?'

ham-fisted (adjective) /hæm ˈfɪstɪd/
clumsy and unskilled.
'The way the government has dealt with this issue has been completely ham-fisted.'

handbags (at dawn) (phrase)
a humorous phrase used to describe a fight in which neither side wants to fight and both fail to inflict any blows upon the other.
'There was a small fight between a couple of the players, but it was just handbags and the game continued soon after.'

handy (adjective) /ˈhændi/
convenient or easy to access.
'It's so handy having a mini-supermarket underneath our flat.'

hanging (adjective) /ˈhæŋɪŋ/ slang
hungover.
'Paulo, you look like you're hanging, mate. Did you get drunk last night?'

hanky-panky (noun) /hæŋkɪ ˈpæŋki/ slang
a slightly old-fashioned humorous term for sexual activity.
'Was there any hanky-panky at the staff party?'

hard (adjective) /hɑːd/ slang
tough and willing to fight.
'You've got to be hard to work as a bouncer.'

hard done by (phrase)
unfairly treated.
'Justina must feel pretty hard done by to not get that promotion. She totally deserved it.'

hard shoulder (noun) /hɑːd ˈʃəʊldə/
the area along the side of a motorway where cars are permitted to stop if they have a problem.
'Let's pull on to the hard shoulder and see what's wrong with the car.'

Harley Street (noun) /ˈhɑːli striːt/
a street in London that is extremely well known and respected for its private medical professionals. It has long been the go-to place for wealthy clients to get advice from Britain's leading surgeons.
'Dr Sing has opened a small practice on Harley Street.'

harp on (about something) (phrasal verb) /hɑːp ˈɒn/
to keep talking about something over and over again so that it becomes annoying to other people.
'Can you stop harping on about how much money you make.'

have a bash (at something) (phrase)
an informal phrase meaning 'to try to do something'.
'I'm going to have a bash at writing a song on the piano.'

TOM'S TIPS

In spoken British English, 'handbag' is actually pronounced /hæmbæg/. This is due to something called assimilation, which is when one sound changes because of a neighbouring sound. In this case, the /n/ becomes an /m/ because of the /b/. Next time you say it, think of bags of ham at dawn! Strange...but useful!

'you're having a laugh'

have a face like the back end of a bus (phrase) rude
an offensive way to say someone is ugly.
'Not only is he a crap reality TV contestant, he also has a face like the back end of a bus.'

have a go at (someone) (phrase)
if you have a go at someone, you criticise them, sometimes unfairly.
'I'm not having a go at you Asha. I'm just saying it would have been nice if you had asked before borrowing my car.'

have a good innings (idiom)
used to say that someone has lived a long and fulfilling life. The phrase has its origins in cricket.
'My grandma died aged 96 and it's fair to say she'd had a good innings.'

have a laugh (phrase)
to have fun or joke around.
'I had such a laugh on Friday night with my uni mates.'

have kittens (phrase)
an informal phrase meaning 'to be very anxious or worried'.
'If we are not back before midnight, my parents will have kittens.'

have (someone) on (phrasal verb) /həv ˈɒn/
to attempt to fool or deceive someone, usually as a joke.
'My sister says she's met George Clooney. I'm sure she's having me on.'

having a laugh (phrase)
used to challenge a ludicrous or insulting thing someone has said.
A – 'How much are these running shoes?'
B – '£299.'
A – 'Are you having a laugh?'

head girl/boy (noun) /hed ˈgɜːl/
the girl or boy who is the leader of the prefects and represents the school at events.
'Shivani has been elected head girl.'

hen do/party (noun) /ˈhen duː/
the celebration a woman has before she gets married.
'So many hen dos go abroad these days.'

het up (adjective) /het ˈʌp/
a slightly old-fashioned term meaning agitated, anxious or angry.
'Don't get so het up over your party, everything will work out fine.'

high street (noun) /ˈhaɪ striːt/
the principal street in the centre of a town that has the main shops and buildings.
'A lot of the shops on the high street have their sales on right now.'

Highway Code (noun) /haɪweɪ ˈkəʊd/
the official set of rules that apply to all road users in the United Kingdom.
'Before you pass your driving test you have to learn everything you can from the Highway Code.'

hire purchase (noun) /haɪə ˈpɜːtʃɪs/
a way to pay for something like a TV or car, in which the purchaser pays a small amount upfront and then regular instalments thereafter.
'We bought this fridge on hire purchase.'

HMRC (abbreviation) /eɪtʃ em ɑː ˈsiː/
short for 'His/Her Majesty's Revenue and Customs'. It is responsible for tax collection.
'Last year I had a rebate from HMRC.'

HMS (abbreviation) /eɪtʃ em ˈes/
short for 'His/Her Majesty's Ship'. It goes before the name of every ship in the British navy.
'One of the biggest tourist attractions in London is HMS Belfast, which is moored near Tower Bridge.'

hoaching (adjective) /ˈhəʊtʃɪŋ/ slang
a Scottish word meaning 'very crowded'.
'The bus to work was hoaching this morning.'

hob (noun) /hɒb/
the surface on top of a cooker on which you heat pans.
'Pop the pan on the hob and get the water to a boil.'

Hogmanay (noun) /hɒgməˈneɪ/
the name used in Scotland for New Year's Eve and the celebrations that take place at that time.
'We're heading to Edinburgh for Hogmanay.'

hole in the wall (noun) /həʊl ɪn ðə ˈwɔːl/
an informal phrase for an ATM (automatic cash dispenser).
'Is there a hole in the wall anywhere around here? I need to get some cash.'

holibobs (noun) /ˈhɒlɪbɒbz/ slang
a very informal alternative for 'holiday'.
'Have you packed for your holibobs yet?'

Holyrood (noun) /ˈhɒliruːd/
a metonym for the Scottish parliament.
'A decision to change the legal drinking age in Scotland will be made by Holyrood this week.'

Home Office (noun) /həʊm ˈɒfɪs/
the UK government department responsible for visas and passports, and for making decisions about people who want to move to the UK from abroad.
'I've applied to the Home Office for a new passport.'

Home Secretary (noun) /həʊm ˈsekrətəri/
the government minister in charge of the Home Office.
'The new Home Secretary is going to announce new visa rules for overseas students.'

hoodie (noun) /ˈhʊdi/
a young person wearing a hooded top who is thought to be up to no good.
'There was a bunch of hoodies hanging around the entrance to the estate, so I decided to take a different route home.'

hooter (noun) /ˈhuːtə/ slang
a nose.
'The first thing you notice about him is his enormous hooter.'

hoover (verb) /ˈhuːvə/
a British trademark, used as a verb, meaning to clean a carpet with a vacuum cleaner.
'Hasan, can you hoover the stairs before the guests arrive?'

horses for courses (idiom)
a phrase used to say that different people like different things, or that different people have different skillsets to other people.
'Half the team like working in the office and half like working from home. It's horses for courses.'

hotchpotch (noun) /ˈhɒtʃpɒtʃ/
a confusing combination of different things.
'The ingredients for this stew are a bit of a hotchpotch from my fridge.'

House of Commons (noun) /haʊs əv ˈkɒmənz/
the lower house of the UK Parliament, in which 650 elected members of parliament meet in Westminster, London.
'You can go to the House of Commons when it is in session. It's a fascinating experience.'

House of Lords (noun) /haʊs əv ˈlɔːdz/
the upper house of the UK Parliament. The members of the Lords are unelected, which is in contrast to the House of Commons. They look at bills that have been approved by the House of Commons.
'The House of Lords is in session this afternoon.'

'how's your father'

housing estate (noun) /ˈhaʊzɪŋ ɪsteɪt/
a large number of homes built at the same time.
'They are planning to build a huge new housing estate on that field over there.'

howay! (exclamation) /hæˈweɪ/
a greeting in the northeast of England.
'Howay man! Did you have a good weekend?'

how long is a piece of string? (phrase)
used to say it is impossible to give an exact answer to a question.
A – *'How much is the Christmas party going to cost?'*
B – *'How long is a piece of string?'*

how's your father (euphemism) /haʊz jə ˈfɑːðə/ rude
an old-fashioned humorous term for sexual intercourse.
'Sounds like they are having a bit of how's your father upstairs!'

HQ (noun) /eɪtʃ ˈkjuː/
an affectionate colloquial term for Twickenham stadium, the home of the England rugby team.
'We're going to HQ for the big match against South Africa on Saturday.'

HRH (abbreviation) /eɪtʃ ɑːr ˈeɪtʃ/
short for 'His/Her Royal Highness', which is a title for some members of the royal family.
'Prince William is HRH the Duke of Cambridge.'

humming (adjective) /ˈhʌmɪŋ/ slang
very bad-smelling.
'Blimey! Your shoes are humming, mate!'

hunky-dory (adjective) /hʌŋki ˈdɔːri/
if everything is hunky-dory, it's fine or going well. Considered a bit old-fashioned.
A – *'How is your dissertation going?'*
B – *'It's hunky-dory at the moment.'*

I

independent school (noun) /ɪndɪˈpendənt skuːl/
another way to say a private school which is fee-paying.
'There is a list of the top 50 independent schools in this week's Sunday Times.'

infant school (noun) /ˈɪnfənt skuːl/
a school for children aged 4–7.
'Jasmine is in her last year of infant school.'

in for a penny (in for a pound) (phrase)
used to express someone's intention to complete a task no matter how hard it might become.
'Well we've started climbing Mount Snowdon and we can't turn back, so in for a penny I guess.'

in (good) nick (phrase)
in good condition or health.
'I'm going to try and sell my old guitar, it's still in pretty good nick.'

innit (contraction) /ˈɪnɪt/ slang
initially a contraction of 'isn't it' but has now become widely used to replace any auxiliary in a question tag. It can also be used to agree with someone. It's extremely informal and mainly used by younger members of society.
'You support Chelsea, innit?' = 'You support Chelsea, don't you?'

'You've been to Poland, innit?' = 'You've been to Poland, haven't you?'

A – 'That gig was amazing.'
B – 'Innit!'

'I often hear people criticise the word "innit" as lazy and incorrect. In my opinion, this couldn't be further from the truth. Language evolves and changes, it's never stagnant. "Innit" is an example of how we are constantly innovating and adapting language to our needs. The grammar of question tags can be complicated, so why not use one word to do the job of many? I think it's kind of genius!'

Teacher Tom

'it's like Piccadilly Circus'

in the buff (idiom) slang
naked.
'Next week, I'm posing for an art class completely in the buff.'

in with a shout (idiom)
having a chance of doing or winning something, e.g. a race or job promotion.
'I think Newcastle are in with a shout of winning the Premier League soon.'

ISA (noun) /ˈaɪsə/
an abbreviation for 'individual savings account'. A tax-free savings account available to people in the UK.
'I'm going to open up an ISA and start saving for a deposit on a house.'

it'd be rude not to (phrase)
a humorous phrase to say yes to a suggestion or proposal.
A – 'Do you fancy getting a drink after work?'
B – 'It'd be rude not to.'

it's like Piccadilly Circus (phrase)
used to say somewhere is extremely busy or crowded.
'I wouldn't go to the station right now. It's like Piccadilly Circus!'

ITV (noun) /aɪ tiː ˈviː/
the first independent television channel in Britain.
'One of the shows that is synonymous with ITV is "Coronation Street".'

J

jacksie (noun) /ˈdʒæksi/ rude
a slang term for a person's bottom.
'Pull your trousers up lad! I can almost see your bloody jacksie!'

Jack-the-lad (noun) /dʒæk ðə ˈlæd/
an overly confident young man who thinks he is attractive and a bit of a bad boy.
'Blimey! Liam has turned into a bit of a Jack-the-lad, hasn't he? He used to be such a lovely boy.'

jammy (adjective) /ˈdʒæmi/
very lucky, often without doing anything to deserve it.
'I can't believe that jammy little brother of mine got an interview at the BBC.'

jar (noun) /dʒɑː/ slang
a drink of beer.
'Shall we get a few jars in the pub before dinner?'

jessie (noun) /ˈdʒesi/ rude
an offensive term for a man who is seen as weak or oversensitive.
'The coach called me a jessie for wearing gloves during football practice.'

jim-jams (noun) /ˈdʒɪm dʒæmz/
a childlike word for 'pyjamas'.
'OK kids, go upstairs and put on your jim-jams.'

jobbie (noun) /ˈdʒɒbi/ slang
a Scottish word for 'excrement'.
'Who's left a wee jobbie in the loo without flushing?'

Jobcentre (noun) /ˈdʒɒb sentə/
the place unemployed people can go to look for work or get advice about employment issues.
'I'm going to pop down to the Jobcentre later and see if they've got any workshops on interview skills.'

'jolly good'

Jobseeker's Allowance (noun) /dʒɒbsi:kəz əˈlaʊəns/
the money the government gives people in search of work.
'Half of the people I went to school with are on Jobseeker's Allowance.'

Joe Bloggs (noun) /dʒəʊ ˈblɒgz/
the name used to represent the average or typical man.
'The challenge for every politician is to try and understand what Joe Bloggs wants.'

johnny (noun) /ˈdʒɒni/ rude
slang for 'condom' (also 'rubber johnny').
'I always get so embarrassed buying johnnies at the chemists.'

jolly (adverb) /ˈdʒɒli/
a slightly posh and old-fashioned way to say 'very'.
'Samantha, that's a jolly nice coat you are wearing. Where did you get it from?'

jolly good (phrase)
an old-fashioned way to express approval or pleasure.
A – 'Simon and Rebecca can come to my graduation, Mum.'
B – 'Oh, jolly good!'

jolly well (phrase)
an old-fashioned phrase used for emphasis, particularly when you are annoyed or angry.
'I should jolly well hope you're sorry after what you did.'

joy (noun) /dʒɔɪ/
success or help, often used in a negative sense.
'Did you have any joy finding that dress you were looking for?'

jumble sale (noun) /ˈdʒʌmbəl seɪl/
a sale, usually for a good cause or charity, in which people sell different types of second-hand items.
'My daughter's school had a jumble sale to help support Oxfam.'

jumped-up (adjective) /dʒʌmpt ˈʌp/
an informal way to describe someone who believes they are more important than they actually are. Used mostly in a work context.
'Peter is such a jumped-up idiot. Why does he try to give me orders when we do the same job?'

junior school (noun) /ˈdʒu:niə sku:l/
a school for children between the ages of seven and eleven (also 'the juniors').
'Once you finish infant school you go on to junior school.'

K

KC (noun) /keɪ ˈsiː/
King's Counsel. A senior barrister.
'Her mother is a KC, so she's decided to study law too.'

kecks (noun) /keks/ slang
trousers or underwear.
'Do you like my new kecks? I got them from Zara.'

kedgeree (noun) /ˈkedʒəri/
a lightly spiced rice dish with smoked fish, onions and eggs. Its origins lie in the Indian dish kitchari. It was adopted by Scottish troops returning home from colonial-era India who yearned for Indian flavours. It's usually served for breakfast or brunch.
'Have you had the kedgeree at The Wolseley? It's delicious.'

keen (adjective) /kiːn/
very interested in something.
'My dad's a really keen gardener, so for his birthday I always get him something related to gardening.'

keen as mustard (phrase)
an informal phrase used to say someone is very enthusiastic.
'The class were keen as mustard to go on their geography field trip with Mr Stone.'

keep your hair on! (phrase)
used to tell someone to calm down and not get so angry.
A – 'Jenny, I can't believe you didn't pay our electricity bill!'
B – 'Keep your hair on! I'll do it tomorrow morning.'

keep your pecker up (phrase)
an informal phrase used to encourage someone to remain positive and cheerful in a difficult time.
'Come on team, keep your peckers up! We can still win this game.'

ken (verb) /ken/
a word used in Scotland to mean 'know'.
'I dinnae ken what you're talking about.'

kerb-crawling (noun) /ˈkɜːb krɔːlɪŋ/
the activity of driving around the streets trying to pick up sex workers.
'The police are trying to reduce kerb-crawling along the Seven Sisters Road.'

kerfuffle (noun) /kəˈfʌfəl/
a big fuss, commotion or excitement about something.
'There was a bit of a kerfuffle as passengers tried to get on the train.'

khazi (noun) /ˈkɑːzi/ slang
an old-fashioned word for 'toilet' (also 'karzi' or 'karzy').
'I'm just popping to the khazi.'

'keep your hair on!'

kickabout (noun) /ˈkɪkəbaʊt/
an informal game of football played just for fun.
'Shall we take the kids to the park and have a kickabout?'

kick (something) into touch (idiom)
to decide not to deal with a problem immediately.
'The government has kicked plans to raise taxes into touch as they seek a general election first.'

kick off (phrasal verb) /kɪk ˈɒf/
to suddenly become angry and start fighting or arguing.
'I think it's going to kick off between the Leeds and Millwall fans.'

kick your heels (idiom)
to be forced to waste time waiting for something or someone.
'I've been kicking my heels since 10 o'clock waiting for my dad to pick me up. He's an hour late.'

kip (noun) /kɪp/ slang
an informal word meaning 'sleep'.
'Don't make too much noise, Grandad's having his afternoon kip.'

kip (verb) /kɪp/ slang
to sleep. It's commonly used in places that aren't designed for sleep, e.g. a sofa or vehicle.
'I managed to kip on the train, so I'm feeling well rested.'

knackered (adjective) /ˈnækəd/ slang
extremely tired, exhausted.
'The kids were absolutely knackered after our day trip to Brighton.'

knackered (adjective) /ˈnækəd/ slang
completely broken or worn out after a lot of use.
'I need a new TV, this one's knackered – it won't even turn on anymore.'

knackers (noun) /ˈnækəz/ rude
a slang term for 'testicles'.
'The ball hit my knackers and I had to sit out of the match for ten minutes.'

knacker's yard (phrase) slang
the place that we say things go when they are too old to be useful.
'I think your car is ready for the knacker's yard, mate!'

knees-up (noun) /ˈni:z ʌp/ slang
a party.
'After the wedding, we all had a knees-up at our house.'

knickers (noun) /ˈnɪkəz/
a term for female underwear.
'I'm just popping to Primark to buy some new knickers.'

knighthood (noun) /ˈnaɪthʊd/
a British rank awarded by the monarch for exceptional service to Britain. It is given to men who can then take the title 'Sir' and women who can then be 'Dame'.
'Knighthoods have been awarded to several politicians this year.'

TOM'S TIPS

The phrase 'knees-up' comes from a popular song from the early 20th century, 'Knees Up Mother Brown'.

‘know your onions’

knob (noun) /nɒb/ rude
a slang term for a penis. It is also used as an insult for someone (also ‘knobhead’).
‘His pants ripped and he accidentally showed everyone his knob.’

knock (verb) /nɒk/
to criticise someone or something.
‘Don’t knock it till you’ve tried it!’

knock around/about (with someone) (phrasal verb) /nɒk əˈraʊnd/
to spend time with someone.
‘Before I moved to London, I used to knock about with a bunch of guys from my secondary school.’

knock (someone) for six (idiom)
an informal phrase used when someone is really shocked or overcome by something, e.g. bad news or an illness (also ‘hit (someone) for six’).
‘That virus really hit me for six. I couldn’t leave my bed!’

knocking shop (noun) /ˈnɒkɪŋ ʃɒp/ rude
a slang term for a brothel.
‘There are quite a few knocking shops right next to where I go to college.’

knock-off (noun) /ˈnɒk ɒf/
a copy or imitation.
‘All the football shirts at this market are knock-offs.’

knock off (phrasal verb) /nɒk ˈɒf/
to stop working at the end of the day.
‘What time do you knock off today?’

(the) knowledge (noun) /ˈnɒlɪdʒ/
the training course a London black cab driver has to take before they get a licence.
‘It takes two years to study for the knowledge.’

know your onions (idiom)
to have a good knowledge of a particular subject.
‘When it comes to world geography Kiko really knows her onions.’

L

la' (noun) /lɑː/ slang
a slang word for 'lad', used instead of 'mate', mainly in Liverpool.
'Alright la', fancy a trip to the seaside tomorrow?'

Labour (noun) /ˈleɪbə/
a British political party. It's full name is the British Labour Party.
'My family have been voting Labour for generations.'

lad (noun) /læd/
a boy or young man.
'Alex Turner is a local lad. He was born here in Sheffield.'

lad (noun) /læd/
a young man who behaves in a way that's considered typical, e.g. gets drunk, chats up girls, fights, etc.
'Declan used to be a bit of a lad before he got married and settled down.'

laddie (noun) /ˈlædi/
a Scottish form of address for a young boy.
'Come here then laddie and help me carry these boxes.'

laddish (adjective) /ˈlædɪʃ/
behaving in a boisterous, loud, sometimes rude way.
'Alex and Julio are lovely guys but when they get together they can be a bit laddish.'

(the) ladies (noun) /ˈleɪdiz/
a polite term for 'women's toilets'.
'I'm just going to pop to the ladies before we leave.'

(the) lads (noun) /lædz/
used to refer to a group of male friends.
'Me and the lads are going to Lisbon for a long weekend.'

lager lout (noun) /ˈlɑːgə laʊt/
a person who gets drunk on beer and behaves obnoxiously or even violently in public.
'Goodness, the lager louts are out in force tonight, aren't they?'

lairy (adjective) /ˈleəri/
noisy and aggressive in an unpleasant way, usually after drinking.
'There were these two guys in the pub getting quite lairy so we decided to leave.'

lamp (verb) /læmp/ slang
to hit someone or something.
'This random geezer got into a fight with my mate and lamped him for no reason.'

Lancashire hotpot (noun) /læŋkəʃə ˈhɒtpɒt/
a stew of lamb and vegetables, topped with sliced potato, which is then cooked in the oven so that the top is crispy. It is said to have been invented by the millworkers of Lancashire.
'The best Lancashire hotpot I've ever had was at a birthday party in Blackburn.'

lashings (noun) /ˈlæʃɪŋz/
a slightly old-fashioned way to say 'lots of', mostly used for food and drink.
'I love my mum's apple crumble with lashings of home-made custard.'

lass (noun) /læs/
a term used mostly in Scotland and the north of England for a girl or young woman (also 'lassie').
'Did you hear Mary and Hamish have had a wee lass? They are going to name her Olive.'

laugh (noun) /lɑ:f/
an informal word that means a source of fun.
'Reggie is a laugh, isn't he? We should invite him to dinner again.'

'last orders'

last orders (noun) /lɑ:st ˈɔ:dəz/
in British pubs the bar person will shout 'last orders', which is an indication that the pub will close soon and that you have a few minutes (usually 15) to buy one more round of drinks.
A – 'What time is last orders?'
B – '11 o'clock.'

laughing gear (noun) /ˈlɑ:fɪŋ gɪə/ slang
the mouth.
'Get your laughing gear around this drink and let's celebrate your birthday in style!'

laugh like a drain (phrase)
to laugh a lot.
'The guy next to me at work laughs like a drain. It is starting to get a bit annoying.'

lay-by (noun) /ˈleɪ baɪ/
a small area beside a road where vehicles can pull in and stop for a short time so that they don't disrupt traffic.
'Why don't we pull into a lay-by and check the map before continuing?'

leave it out (phrase)
used to tell someone to stop doing something, e.g. teasing or nagging.
A – 'Come on son, when are you going to get a good job?'
B – 'Dad, leave it out! I'll get one as soon as the summer is over.'

ledge (noun) /ledʒ/ slang
short for 'legend'. It's used to describe someone you think is great, often a friend or loved one.
'Thanks for agreeing to pick up the kids today. You are an absolute ledge.'

lefty (noun) /ˈlefti/
someone who supports left-wing politics (also 'leftie').
'My dad thinks I'm a complete lefty just because I think they should raise the minimum wage.'

lefty (noun) /ˈlefti/
someone who has a dominant left hand (short for 'left-handed').
'I'm the only lefty in my family; my parents and brothers are right-handed.'

leg it (phrase)
an informal phrase meaning to run as quickly as possible, usually away from something.
'Franco legged it home from school as soon as the bell rang.'

let (verb) /let/
to allow someone to rent your house or flat.
'Are you thinking of letting your flat when you move to Kuala Lumpur?'

Liberal Democrats (noun) /lɪbərəl ˈdeməkræts/
a British political party (also 'Lib Dems').
'I voted for the Liberal Democrats in the last general election.'

lido (noun) /ˈliːdəʊ/
an outdoor swimming pool.
'Every Friday evening during the summer I try and do a few laps at Brockwell Lido.'

lie-down (noun) /laɪ ˈdaʊn/
a short rest, usually horizontally on a sofa or bed.
'Do you want to have a quick lie-down before we go out for dinner?'

lie-in (noun) /laɪ ˈɪn/
the act of staying in bed longer than is usual.
'I get up so early during the week so it's always a treat to have a lie-in on Saturdays.'

lift (noun) /lɪft/
a machine that takes people up and down in buildings between floors ('elevator' in American English).
'Have you noticed that Niall never takes the lift back to our office – he always walks up the stairs.'

like a headless chicken (phrase)
used to describe someone who has lost their composure, self-control and ability to think sensibly.
'After Arsenal went 4–0 down the players just ran around like headless chickens.'

like the clappers (phrase) slang
very fast.
'When Sally wants to, she can run like the clappers.'

lippy (noun) /ˈlɪpi/
a shortened form of 'lipstick'.
'Sweetie, can I borrow your lippy?'

lippy (adjective) /ˈlɪpi/
if you are lippy, you speak to someone in a disrespectful way.
'The kids in my class are so lippy to the teacher.'

listed building/structure (noun) /lɪstɪd ˈbɪldɪŋ/
a building that is deemed significant for historical or architectural reasons and cannot be changed or knocked down.
'I didn't know that the crossing on Abbey Road where the Beatles took their famous photo is a listed structure.'

Liverpudlian (noun) /livəˈpʌdliən/
someone from the city of Liverpool.
'My dad's a Liverpudlian but he's lived in Dorset for the last decade.'

local (noun) /ˈləʊkəl/
the pub you visit the most that is near your home. Because pub culture is very important in British life, traditionally everyone would have a 'local' they always drank in.
'Come round to my house for some dinner and then we can pop down to my local for a couple of pints.'

loch (noun) /lɒx/
a Scottish word for 'lake'.
'We went to Loch Lomond for my husband's fortieth birthday.'

lodger (noun) /ˈlɒdʒə/
someone who rents a room in a house where the owner is living.
'Growing up, we always used to have lodgers living with us.'

'There have been many great songs about London like "London Calling" by The Clash and "LDN" by Lily Allen, but none of them has the old-school charm of the music hall classic "Maybe It's Because I'm a Londoner". Take a walk along the South Bank whistling this tune and you'll feel like a local in no time.'

Teacher Tom

lollipop lady/man (noun) /ˈlɒlipɒp leɪdi/
a person whose job it is to help children cross the street, usually next to a school.
'My gran was a lollipop lady for 40 years.'

Londoner (noun) /ˈlʌndənə/
someone from London.
'I moved to London three years ago and I've barely met any Londoners.'

loo (noun) /luː/
an informal word for 'toilet'.
'Kids, make sure you go to the loo before we leave the house.'

lose the plot (idiom)
if you lose the plot, you are no longer able to understand a situation and deal with it.
'After his wife left him, Fergus completely lost the plot for a while.'

lounge (noun) /laʊndʒ/
another word for 'sitting room'.
'Let's go into the lounge and open the Christmas presents there.

love (noun) /lʌv/
an affectionate term for someone (also 'luv').
'Alright love, how was your day?'

'lovely jubbly'

lovely (adjective) /ˈlʌvli/
enjoyable or pleasing.
'We had such a lovely weekend in Harrogate. I can't wait to go back.'

lovely jubbly (phrase)
an expression used to express happiness or approval. It was made famous in a TV show called 'Only Fools and Horses'.
A – 'OK, I've ordered the pizzas. They should be here in 20 minutes'.
B – 'Lovely jubbly.'

lucky dip (noun) /lʌki ˈdɪp/
a game in which participants select a prize from a container of prizes all concealed from view.
'There's always a lucky dip at the staff Christmas party.'

lughole (noun) /ˈlʌghəʊl/ slang
a humorous term for an ear.
'I think you kids need to clean your lugholes because you didn't hear a word I just said, did you?

lurgy (noun) /ˈlɜːgi/
an unspecific illness that isn't very serious but is easy to catch.
'Little Freddy has caught the lurgy from one of the kids at nursery.'

lush (adjective) /lʌʃ/ slang
very impressive or desirable. Most commonly used in England (also 'gert lush' mainly in the West Country).
'Wow! That birthday cake looks lush.'

M

M1 (noun) /em ˈwʌn/
the main motorway in England connecting London to the north of England or, if you prefer, the north of England to London.
'Let's take the M1 north until junction 25.'

Maccy D's (noun) /mæki ˈdiːz/ slang
McDonald's, the fast-food chain (also 'Maccies').
'Let's get a Maccy D's on the way home.'

Mackem (noun) /ˈmækəm/
someone from Sunderland.
'Mackems and Geordies have a big footballing rivalry.'

made up (adjective) /meɪd ˈʌp/
an informal alternative to 'happy'.
'I'm absolutely made up you can come to my graduation.'

mad for it (phrase)
a phrase coined in Manchester to mean you are full of enthusiasm to do something.
'Let's go out lads, I'm mad for it!'

maisonette (noun) /meɪzəˈnet/
a small flat with two floors that is part of a larger block of flats but has its own entrance.
'I grew up in a maisonette, just a street away from the Fulham stadium.'

make a pig's ear out of (something) (idiom)
to do something in a really bad or unskilled way.
'I tried to bake croissants this morning, but I made an absolute pig's ear of it.'

make a song and dance (about something) (idiom)
to make an unnecessary fuss about something.
'Lucy made a real song and dance about having to split the bill at dinner last night.'

mam (noun) /mæm/
a variation of 'mum', used in the north of England.
'My mam is set to retire this year after working for 26 years at our local primary school.'

Mancunian (noun) /mæŋˈkjuːniən/
someone from Manchester (also 'Manc').
'My ex-boyfriend was a Mancunian and supported Manchester City.'

Manny (noun) /ˈmæni/ slang
a short form of 'Manchester'.
'I'm going back up to Manny on Sunday.'

manor (noun) /ˈmænə/ slang
an area or neighbourhood.
'There aren't many nice shops or restaurants in my manor.'

mardy (adjective) /ˈmɑːdi/ slang
moody or sulky, mainly used in northern England.
'My brother always gets really mardy if his football team loses.'

TOM'S TIPS

Marmite – a savoury spread made from yeast extract – is Britain's most divisive food. There was a long-running ad campaign with the slogan 'You either love it or you hate it!'. I really recommend trying it at least once in your life. There's also a snack called Twiglets, which has a very similar flavour. In Australia, they have their own version called Vegemite.

Marmite (noun) /ˈmɑːmaɪt/
a well-known savoury spread made from yeast extract that's most commonly eaten on toast.
'I got my mother-in-law to try Marmite and she loved it.'

marmite (adjective) /ˈmɑːmaɪt/
if something is marmite, people either love it or hate it. This concept comes from the fact that Marmite has a very strong taste, which can divide opinion.
'That new character in "EastEnders" is totally marmite. Half my friends can't stand him and the other half adore him.'

mash (noun) /mæʃ/
short form of 'mashed potato'.
'Can I have pie and mash, please?'

mate (noun) /meɪt/
an informal word for 'friend'.
'I've got all my mates coming round for the England game.'

mates' rates (noun) /ˈmeɪts reɪts/
a preferential price or rate because you are friends with someone.
'Why don't you stay in my spare room and I'll give you mates' rates?'

MBE (noun) /em biː ˈiː/
Member of the Order of the British Empire. It is a British honour given by the monarch for exceptional service and contributions to Britain.
'Shahid Khan was given an MBE for services to his local community.'

meat and two veg (phrase) rude
a humorous term for a man's genitals.
'Have you ever had a ball kicked into your meat and two veg? It's bloody painful!'

melt (noun) /melt/ slang
someone that acts in a pathetic or wimpy way.
'Seamus has got no chance with Laura. He's too much of a melt.'

mental (adjective) /ˈmentəl/
slang
crazy. It can be used positively or negatively for someone or something depending on the context.
'The ending of the film is absolutely mental! Characters get killed off left, right and centre.'

menty B (noun) /mənti ˈbiː/ slang
a very informal way to refer to the concept of a mental breakdown. It's used to provide a softer phrase that helps people talk about the issue of mental health more freely.
'I've got so much going on in my head at the moment, I feel like I'm on the verge of a menty B.'

Metropolitan Police (noun) /metrəˈpɒlɪtən pəˈliːs/
London's police force (also 'the Met').
'The Metropolitan Police are responsible for policing 32 London boroughs.'

MI5 (noun) /em aɪ ˈfaɪv/
the United Kingdom's domestic security service responsible for protecting British political and economic interests as well as countering terrorism and espionage within the UK.
'I'd love to apply for a job at MI5, but I don't think I've got the necessary skills.'

MI6 (noun) /em aɪ ˈsɪks/
formally known as the Secret Intelligence Service, MI6 is responsible for foreign-intelligence gathering to help protect the United Kingdom's national security.
'Have you seen the MI6 headquarters? It's an incredible building.'

minger (noun) /ˈmɪŋə/ slang
a rude, derogatory term for someone ugly.
'There's no way I'd go on a date with him, he's an absolute minger.'

minging (adjective) /ˈmɪŋɪŋ/ slang
ugly, or smelly and unpleasant.
'Your shoes are minging. Please give them a good clean before bringing them inside the house.'

mint (adjective) /mɪnt/ slang
good or excellent.
'Your new speakers are mint, mate. Where did you get them from?'

'Brits have a gift for creating playful abbreviations like "tommy K" (tomato ketchup) or "savvy B" (Sauvignon blanc). You'll notice a few more in this section that refer to more difficult topics, e.g. "menty B" (mental breakdown) and "cozzie livs" (the cost of living crisis). While not everyone likes using these phrases, I think they do serve a real purpose in our lexicon. They help people talk about hard things (mental health/poverty) in softer ways. If that encourages people to discuss these things more openly and freely, that's got to be a positive, in my view.'

Teacher Tom

minted (adjective) /ˈmɪntɪd/ slang
very wealthy.
'I didn't realise just how minted Alison's parents are!'

mi'sen (pronoun) /mɪˈsen/
a way to say 'myself', used in the north of England.
A – 'Have you got an iPhone?'
B – 'I haven't got one mi'sen, but my son has.'

misery guts (noun) /ˈmɪzəri gʌts/
someone who is quite negative, miserable and likes to complain.
'I love spending time with Olivia, but her husband Noah can be a bit of a misery guts.'

mockney (noun) /ˈmɒkni/
someone who uses the pronunciation features of Cockney even though they are not a Cockney. They might do this to fit into a social situation or appear 'cool'. It is usually done by someone from the upper-middle classes trying to be seen as one of the common people.
'People often accuse Jamie Oliver of being a mockney.'

money for old rope (phrase)
money that you receive for doing something you consider easy.
'Honestly tutoring maths to primary school kids is money for old rope.'

'money for old rope'

mither (verb) /ˈmaɪðə/ slang
a northern English word meaning 'complain'.
'My neighbour has been mithering about our dog barking.'

mizzle (noun) /ˈmɪzəl/
light rain (mainly used in England in the North, the Midlands and the Southwest).
'They've forecasted a little mizzle this afternoon.'

monkey (noun) /ˈmʌŋki/ slang
London slang for £500.
'I can't believe that car only costs a monkey!'

monk on (phrase) slang
a northern English phrase meaning 'annoyed' or 'in a bad mood'.
'Don't get a monk on just because I don't want to watch the same film as you.'

‘hello my old mucker’

morris dancing (noun) /ˈmɒrɪs dɑ:nsɪŋ/
a traditional English folk dance by a group of people dressed in a special costume, usually with bells attached.
‘If you visit Broadstairs Folk Week, you’ll see lots of morris dancing.’

motorway (noun) /ˈməʊtəweɪ/
a road with several lanes on which cars can drive at high speed. In Britain, they are named M and then a number, e.g. M25.
‘I think we have to take the M6 to get to Manchester.’

move the goalposts (idiom)
change the rules or requirements while someone is trying to do something.
‘Our marketing team had come up with a great strategy for the year, but then the CEO changed her mind and moved the goalposts, so now we need to rethink the whole thing.’

MP (noun) /em ˈpi:/
Member of Parliament. A person who has been elected to become a politician and represent their constituency.
‘A large number of Lib Dem MPs voted against the government.’

muck about/around (phrasal verb) /mʌk əˈbaʊt/
to waste time and behave in a silly way.
‘Kids! Stop mucking about and get back to your homework.’

mucker (noun) /ˈmʌkə/ slang
a slightly old-fashioned slang term for ‘friend’.
‘Hello my old mucker, come in and I’ll make you a cuppa.’

muck in (phrasal verb) /mʌk ˈɪn/
to share tasks that need to be done.
‘If everyone mucks in with the cleaning, we can all go home early.’

muck up (phrasal verb) /mʌk ˈʌp/
an informal phrase meaning to make a mistake that means something is spoiled.
‘Our new drummer keeps on mucking up in band practice. It’s so frustrating.’

mudlarking (noun) /ˈmʌdlɑ:kɪŋ/
the act of searching for objects of value in soft wet ground, i.e. on the banks of rivers.
‘My grandpa used to take me mudlarking every Sunday on the banks of the River Thames.’

mufti day (noun) /ˈmʌfti deɪ/
a school day in which pupils can wear whatever clothes they like and are not required to wear their school uniforms.
‘I always loved mufti day so I could go to school wearing my favourite purple dress.’

mug (noun) /mʌg/ slang
an insulting word to describe someone as a ‘fool’ or ‘idiot’.
‘Look at that mug over there trying to park his car! The man can’t drive.’

muggins (noun) /ˈmʌgɪnz/
a humorous way to refer to yourself when you’ve been stupid or unfairly treated.
‘I guess muggins over here will have to look after the dog if you are away this weekend.’

mug (someone) off (phrasal verb) /mʌg 'ɒf/ slang
to make someone look an idiot or fool.
'Did you text your ex-girlfriend last night? Don't try and mug me off, I know you did!'

mummy's boy (noun) /'mʌmiz bɔɪ/
a boy or man who is severely influenced by his mother and does what she says.
'Don't you think Sammy is a bit of a mummy's boy? He doesn't seem to have a mind of his own.'

Munro (noun) /mʌn'rəʊ/
a word used in Scotland for mountains that are above 3,000 feet high.
'There are 282 Munros in Scotland.'

munter (noun) /'mʌntə/ rude
a derogatory word for someone ugly.
A – 'Stefan, why have you only ever gone out with munters?'
B – 'Get lost!'

muppet (noun) /'mʌpɪt/ slang
a foolish person.
'I'm such a muppet! I've left my laptop at home so I can't access my emails today.'

mushy peas (noun) /mʌʃi 'pi:z/
a side dish made of mashed-up marrowfat peas, usually served with fish and chips.
'I'll have a large cod and chips with a side of mushy peas, please.'

muso (noun) /'mju:zəʊ/
someone who is really into music.
'I've never met a bigger muso than Nick. He knows his stuff, particularly 90s hip-hop.'

mustard (adjective) /'mʌstəd/ slang
excellent or great.
'The new iPhone is absolutely mustard.'

mustn't grumble (phrase)
a humorous phrase used to say that life is OK and you have no cause to complain.
A – 'How's life, Harry?'
B – 'Oh you know how it is, mustn't grumble.'

mutton dressed as lamb (phrase) rude
a derogatory term for an older or middle-aged woman* who wears clothes that might be considered more suitable for a younger woman.
*notice there is no word for an older man who does something similar.
'I feel a bit like mutton dressed as lamb in this skirt. What do you think?'

mutt's nuts (phrase) rude
a slightly rude informal phrase meaning 'brilliant' or 'fantastic' (synonym of 'dog's bollocks').
'This sausage roll is the mutt's nuts.'

my lover (phrase) /maɪ 'lʌvə/
an affectionate term used in southwest England. Don't worry, it doesn't mean they like you romantically!
'Alright my lover! How's life treating you?'

N

nae (adverb) /neɪ/
Scottish for 'no'.
'I'll give you a lift to the station, it's nae bother.'

naff (adjective) /næf/ slang
without style or class.
'Look at that naff jacket that politician is wearing! Don't you think he should have worn something more formal?'

naff off (phrasal verb) /næf ˈɒf/ slang
used to say 'go away' in a rude way.
A – 'When are you guys going to finally get married?'
B – 'Oh naff off! Why does everyone keep asking us that?'

nah (adverb) /nɑ:/ slang
a spoken variation of 'no' used in many British English accents.
A – 'Have you got a phone charger I can borrow?'
B – 'Nah mate, sorry.'

'nah mate'

nan (noun) /næn/
an informal word for 'grandmother'.
'My nan makes the best chocolate cake in Greater Manchester.'

narked (adjective) /nɑ:kt/ slang
angry about something.
'Don't get narked but I think Rani has stolen your last piece of chocolate.'

narky (adjective) /ˈnɑ:ki/
easily annoyed.
'There's no need to get narky! All I said was that I liked Pablo's cooking more than yours because he's a professional chef.'

National Curriculum (noun) /næʃənəl kəˈrɪkjʊləm/
almost all state schools in England and Wales follow the National Curriculum, which is an established course of study for each subject between the ages of 5 and 16.
'There are plans to change the National Curriculum next year.'

National Grid (noun) /næʃənəl ˈgrɪd/
the system of power lines that connect across Britain.
'The National Grid was established to make sure the power supply around Britain was always met.'

National Insurance Number (noun) /næʃənəl ɪnˈʃɔ:rəns nʌmbə/
a number given to every UK citizen to help with the administration of tax and social security.
'I can never remember my National Insurance Number.'

‘nice one!’

National Living Wage (noun) /næʃənəl lɪvɪŋ ˈweɪdʒ/
a statutory minimum wage given to all workers 21 years old and above.
‘The government has just raised the National Living Wage by 5%.’

National Minimum Wage (noun) /næʃənəl mɪnɪməm ˈweɪdʒ/
a statutory minimum wage given to all school leavers aged 16 and over. The amount varies depending on how old you are. Usually just referred to as ‘minimum wage’.
‘At the moment my daughter is earning minimum wage but hopefully she’ll get a promotion and earn a little more soon.’

National Trust (noun) /næʃənəl ˈtrʌst/
a British organisation that is concerned with maintaining and preserving historic buildings and natural habitats in England, Northern Ireland and Wales.
‘The National Trust does an amazing job preserving historic buildings.’

neck (verb) /nek/ slang
to drink the entire contents of your glass in one go.
‘I bet you can’t neck that pint of Guinness.’

neeps and tatties (noun) /ni:pz ən ˈtætiz/
Scottish side dishes served with haggis, consisting of mashed turnips and potatoes.
‘You’ve always got to have neeps and tatties with haggis.’

new town (noun) /ˈnju: taʊn/
a town designed and built to create a new place for people to live, usually on land that wasn’t used before. English examples include Welwyn Garden City and Milton Keynes.
‘New towns like Milton Keynes were built in the 1960s.’

(the) NHS (noun) /en eɪtʃ ˈes/
the National Health Service. The service in the UK that provides free medical care to everyone living here.
‘The NHS was founded in 1948.’

nice one! (phrase)
used to show approval.
A – ‘We’ve just been invited to Kaz’s wedding.’
B – ‘Nice one!’

nick (verb) /nɪk/ slang
to steal something.
‘When I was 12 I nicked a packet of sweets from my local corner shop.’

(the) nick (noun) /nɪk/ slang
prison.
‘He’s been in the nick for as long as I can remember.’

niggle (noun) /ˈnɪgəl/
a small pain, annoyance or worry.
‘Our captain has got a little niggle in his ankle, but he should be able to play on Saturday.’

niggle (verb) /ˈnɪgəl/
if something is niggling at you, it causes you worry, annoyance or pain.
'What my boss said to me about my future at the company is really niggling away at me.'

nip (verb) /nɪp/
to go somewhere quickly and for a short time. It can be used with lots of different prepositions.
'I'm just going to nip downstairs and put the kettle on. Do you want a drink?'

nippy (adjective) /ˈnɪpi/ slang
chilly or cold.
'It's really warm during the day, but then it gets a bit nippy in the evening.'

nippy (adjective) /ˈnɪpi/
able to change direction quickly and easily.
'Wrexham have just signed a nippy winger from Porto.'

Northerner (noun) /ˈnɔːðənə/
someone from the north of England.
'I think Northerners are much more friendly than Southerners.'

nosh (noun) /nɒʃ/ slang
food.
'Where's the best place to get some good nosh around here?'

nosy (noun) /ˈnəʊzi/
a look around a location because you are curious to see what it is like.
'I'd love to have a nosy around Buckingham Palace and see how the King lives.'

nosy parker (noun) /nəʊzi ˈpɑːkə/
someone who is overly interested in other people's business or affairs.
'Why do you want to know who I was speaking to? You're such a nosy parker!'

not a patch on (phrase)
not nearly as good as something.
'I like soy milk but it's not a patch on oat milk.'

not a sausage (phrase)
a humorous, slightly old-fashioned phrase meaning 'nothing'.
A – 'Do you have any coins I can borrow to feed the parking meter?'
B – 'Sorry mate, I haven't got a sausage.'

not cricket (phrase)
an old-fashioned phrase to describe something that is not honest or moral.
'The way that newspaper secretly recorded people's phone calls is just not cricket!'

not give a monkey's (about something) (phrase)
if you don't give a monkey's about something, you're not worried about it or don't care.
'I don't give a monkey's if you're hungover, we have to go to this brunch with my friends.'

not half (phrase)
an informal phrase used to emphasise a positive statement.
'It wasn't half hot in Mallorca.' (meaning 'It was very hot in Mallorca')
'He doesn't half look like his dad.' (meaning 'He looks a lot like his dad')

not know your arse from your elbow (phrase) rude
to be incompetent, stupid and unable to do simple tasks.
'Don't ask Frank to build your wardrobe. He doesn't know his arse from his elbow.'

'not my cup of tea'

not my cup of tea (phrase)
if something is not your cup of tea, it isn't something you like.
A – 'Have you ever gone fishing, Gabriela?'
B – 'Yeah, I went once with my dad, but to be honest, it's not really my cup of tea.'

not on (phrase)
not acceptable or reasonable.
'The way your boss talks to you is just not on.'

not on your nelly! (phrase)
an old-fashioned phrase meaning 'no way' or 'absolutely not'.
A – 'Mum, can we get a big bottle of juice to share?'
B – 'Not on your nelly!'

not short of a bob or two (phrase)
a slightly old-fashioned informal phrase used to say someone is wealthy.
'She's obviously not short of a bob or two if she's living in a two-bedroom flat in Mayfair.'

nowt (pronoun) /naʊt/
a word used in the north of England to replace 'nothing'.
'I've got nowt in my fridge except for milk and cheese.'

now then! (expression) /ˈnaʊ ðen/
a way to greet someone in some parts of the north of England.
'Now then Andy, how are you lad?'

Number 10 (noun) /nʌmbə ˈten/
10 Downing Street, the official home of the Prime Minister (also 'No. 10').
'The Prime Minister left Number 10 early this morning in preparation for the G7 summit.'

numpty (noun) /ˈnʌmpti/ slang
a stupid person.
'You are such a numpty. Why did you leave the front door unlocked?'

nut (verb) /nʌt/ slang
to headbutt someone, i.e. use your head to hit someone violently.
'The only time I have seen a fight, I saw this super-drunk guy nut this other man.'

nutmeg (noun) /ˈnʌtmeg/
the act of putting a ball between someone's legs, usually used in the context of football.
'That nutmeg by Moore was pure class.'

nutmeg (verb) /ˈnʌtmeg/
to put a ball between someone's legs, usually used in the context of football.
'Did you see the way he nutmegged the defender?'

nutter (noun) /ˈnʌtə/ slang
a disapproving term for someone whose behaviour you find strange, wild or crazy.
'You are a nutter if you think I'm going to go skydiving with you.'

NVQ (noun) /en viː ˈkjuː/
National Vocational Qualification. A skills-focused qualification.
'My nephew is studying an NVQ in plumbing.'

O

OBE (noun) /əʊ biː ˈiː/
Officer of the Order of the British Empire. It is a British honour given by the monarch for exceptional service and contributions to Britain.
'Several players from the England Lionesses team received OBEs.'

odds and sods (noun) /ɒdz ən ˈsɒdz/
miscellaneous items.
A – 'Have you finally unpacked and settled into your new flat?'
B – 'Almost! I've got a few odds and sods in a box I need to unpack.'

off (adjective) /ɒf/
rude.
'I just think it's a bit off that he didn't get you a Valentine's card.'

off (your) face/tits/pickle (phrase) rude
a slang term for very drunk or under the influence of drugs. 'Off one's face' and 'pickle' are informal but neutral, whereas 'off one's tits' is considered rude.
'Toby was off his face last night, as usual.'

Official Secrets Act (noun) /əfɪʃəl ˈsiːkrəts ækt/
a law in the UK forbidding government workers from sharing secret information about the government.
'When she joined the Ministry of Defence she had to sign the Official Secrets Act.'

off-licence (noun) /ˈɒf laɪsəns/
a shop that sells alcohol (also 'offy' and 'offie').
'All the off-licences in the town have closed down.'

off the back of a lorry (phrase)
if something is off the back of a lorry, it has been acquired dishonestly and therefore is being sold for a cheaper price.
'There's a market in London where everything is off the back of a lorry.'

off (your) trolley/rocker (phrase) slang
an informal way to describe someone as crazy.
'You must be off your trolley if you think I'm going to do your homework for you.'

Ofsted (noun) /ˈɒfsted/
this is the short name for the non-ministerial department of the government that deals with standards in education. All schools in England have Ofsted inspections to determine if they meet the required standard.
'My school just had an Ofsted inspection and everyone was on their best behaviour.'

oh go on then! (phrase)
used to say yes to an offer you know you should probably say no to. For example, an extra chocolate biscuit or glass of wine.
A – 'Would you like another glass of wine?'
B – 'Oh go on then!'

oh my giddy aunt! (exclamation) /əʊ maɪ ˈɡɪdi ɑːnt/
an old-fashioned way to show surprise.
A – 'Ali and Rebecca are getting divorced!'
B – 'Oh my giddy aunt! I can't believe it.'

Oi! (interjection) /ɔɪ/
used to get someone's attention.
'Oi kids, come down here and finish your dinner.'

old bean (noun) /əʊld ˈbiːn/
an old-fashioned term of endearment.
'Good morning old bean, how are you today?'

old bill (noun) /əʊld ˈbɪl/ slang
the police.
'I've called the old bill so they should be here shortly.'

Old Firm (noun) /əʊld ˈfɜːm/
a term used to refer to the two biggest football clubs in Scotland: Glasgow Rangers and Glasgow Celtic.
'My dream is to attend an Old Firm derby one day.'

old girl/boy (noun) /əʊld ˈgɜːl/
a former student of a school.
'They've invited all the old girls back to my school for a reunion in the summer.'

omnishambles (noun) /ˈɒmniʃæmbəlz/
a situation that has been completely mismanaged by a large number of people or departments. This word derives from a British TV show called 'The Thick of It'.
'Let's be honest, Brexit was a complete omnishambles.'

one-armed bandit (noun) /wʌn ɑːmd ˈbændɪt/ slang
a slot machine with a large handle on the side you pull down. It's a form of gambling.
'Whenever I come to this pub, Rob is always on the one-armed bandit.'

one-off (noun) /wʌn ˈɒf/
if something is a one-off, it is only done once. If someone is a one-off, they are unique and special in some way.
'I can babysit tonight, but it's a one-off. I'm not great with kids.'

one of the lads (phrase)
a man (or woman) who is accepted as part of a group of men who behave in a way that is seen as masculine.
'To be honest, even though I was in all the school football teams, I was never really one of the lads.'

ono (abbreviation)
stands for 'or nearest offer' and is used in informal adverts where people are trying to sell something. They set the price they want and write 'ono'. It's an invitation to offer an amount you think is reasonable. It is used in written English rather than spoken English.
'Bike for sale, 2 years old. £80 ono.'

on the blink (phrase)
not working or functioning properly.
'My hot water is on the blink at the moment, so I'm showering at the gym every day.'

'Oi oi mate!'

'our kid'

on the piss/razz/lash (phrase) rude
a slang phrase that means drinking a lot of alcohol while out in pubs and bars. 'On the piss/lash' are considered more impolite than 'on the razz'.
'That's the uni rugby team over there. They're clearly on the lash tonight after winning the league.'

on the pull (phrase) slang
if you are on the pull, you are actively looking for someone to kiss or have sexual relations with.
'Let's go on the pull tonight and see if we can have some fun.'

on the razzle/tiles (phrase) slang
going out and enjoying yourself, i.e. drinking, partying, etc.
A – 'Where's Charlotte tonight?'
B – 'She's out on the razzle with her uni mates.'

Open University (noun) /əʊpən juːnɪˈvɜːsɪti/
a British university in which students study from home and submit their work online or by post. It was designed for older people who had never gone to university (also known as the 'OU').
'I did a course with the OU last year and absolutely loved it.'

OTT (adjective) /əʊ tiː ˈtiː/
stands for 'over the top'. It's used to describe something that is excessive or extreme
'Breaking up with Vladimir because of his affair is one thing, but locking him out of the house as well seems a bit OTT.'

our kid (phrase)
an affectionate term originally used for your younger brother or sister, but now used for anyone close like a younger relative or close friend. Mainly used in the north of England.
'Our kid's going to join us for a walk later.'

out of pocket (phrase)
having less money than you did before an activity.
'Thousands of shareholders could be left out of pocket if the company goes bankrupt.'

out out (adverb) /ˈaʊt aʊt/
if you go 'out out', you have a very big night out, i.e. stay out late going to bars or clubs.
'The last time I was in Brighton, I went out out and I had to spend the rest of the weekend in bed with the worst hangover.'

own-brand (adjective) /əʊn ˈbrænd/
used to describe a product a supermarket produces and sells with its own name on it, e.g. Tesco soap (not another brand's soap).
'Can you taste the difference between own-brand cereals and more well-known brands?'

owt (pronoun) /aʊt/
a word used in the north of England to replace 'anything'.
'Do you want owt from the shops?'

Oxbridge (noun) /ˈɒksbrɪdʒ/
a term used to refer to the universities of Oxford and Cambridge.
'20% of students from this school go on to get places at Oxbridge.'

Oz (noun) /ɒz/
a short form of 'Australia' (also written 'Auz' and 'Aus').
'She grew up in Oz, but moved to the UK when she was eight.'

P

P45 (noun) /piː fɔːti ˈfaɪv/
the official document issued to someone when they have stopped working at a company.
'Your P45 will be sent to you in the next few weeks.'

P60 (noun) /piː ˈsɪksti/
the end-of-tax-year certificate showing someone's taxable income and deductions made by PAYE.
'Can you please send us a copy of your P60 and proof of address?'

PA (noun) /piː ˈeɪ/
abbreviation of 'personal assistant'. This is someone who helps a person of authority with their basic tasks, like arranging meetings, etc.
'I worked as a PA in the city for many years before leaving to start my company.'

packed lunch (noun) /pækt ˈlʌntʃ/
a meal prepared at home and taken to school, work or on an excursion.
'My dad used to make the most delicious packed lunches.'

pack it in! (phrase)
an exclamation used to tell someone to stop doing something, usually because it's annoying you.
'Kids, can you pack it in! I've had enough of you running around screaming.'

pain in the arse/neck (phrase) rude
a way to say something or someone is very annoying.
'This weekend's Tube closures are a real pain in the arse.'

Pancake Day (noun) /ˈpænkeɪk deɪ/
a Tuesday in February/March when people traditionally eat pancakes before a period of fasting called Lent. Although it is associated with Christianity, it is widely celebrated by people who aren't of the Christian faith in the UK (also 'Shrove Tuesday').
'This year Pancake Day falls on my birthday, so we're having pancakes instead of birthday cake.'

panny D (noun) /pæni ˈdiː/ slang
a very informal way to refer to the Covid-19 pandemic. It is used by some as a softer way to talk about a difficult and traumatic time.
'Where were you living during the panny D?'

pantomime (noun) /ˈpæntəmaɪm/
a traditional theatrical performance around Christmas time. It always involves a well-known story like Robin Hood or Aladdin, with lots of topical jokes, colourful costumes and music (also 'panto').
'Every year my family go to the pantomime at the Hackney Empire. It's a bit of a tradition.'

'pack it in!'

pants (adjective) /pænts/ slang
not very good.
'The music at the club last night was pants.'

parky (adjective) /ˈpɑ:ki/ slang
cold.
'It's a bit parky today, I might go home and get my jumper.'

PAYE (abbreviation) /pi: eɪ waɪ ˈi:/
pay-as-you-earn tax system used in the UK.
'I have always paid my tax with PAYE but now I'm self-employed I have to do a tax return myself.'

PC (noun) /pi: ˈsi:/
police constable.
'PC Robinson chased the burglar out of the house and into the garden.'

peaky (adjective) /ˈpi:ki/
pale and unwell.
'You look a bit peaky, love. Do you want to have a lie-down?'

(go) pear-shaped (phrase)
if a plan or activity goes pear-shaped, it goes wrong.
'My plans to go travelling over the summer went pear-shaped when I broke my leg.'

pea-souper (noun) /pi: ˈsu:pə/ slang
an old-fashioned term for a very thick fog.
'What a shame we can't see Big Ben, it's a real pea-souper today.'

peckish (adjective) /ˈpekɪʃ/
a little bit hungry.
'I'm always a little peckish around 11 o'clock in the morning.'

peely-wally (adjective) /ˈpi:li ˈwæli/
a Scottish word meaning 'pale' or 'ill-looking'.
'You lads are looking a wee bit peely-wally this morning. Were you out late last night?'

pelican crossing (noun) /pelɪkən ˈkrɒsɪŋ/
a pedestrian crossing operated by lights.
'Don't cross there guys! Let's walk to the pelican crossing, it's much safer.'

pelters (noun) /ˈpeltəz/ slang
an informal word for 'criticism'.
'I've received pelters online for saying kimchi is overrated.'

pet (noun) /pet/
an affectionate term for someone, most commonly heard in the north of England.
'Alright pet, how's your mum doing?'

petrol station (noun) /ˈpetrəl steɪʃən/
the place where you can buy petrol for your vehicle. There is usually a small shop too.
'Excuse me, do you know where the nearest petrol station is?'

PGCE (noun) /pi: dʒi: si: ˈi:/
an abbreviation of 'Postgraduate Certificate in Education'. This is the qualification required to teach children in mainstream education.
'So many of my friends are doing the PGCE right now.'

pie (verb) /paɪ/ slang
to break up with someone.
'He got pied by his girlfriend via text message.'

pie and mash (noun) /paɪ ən ˈmæʃ/
the traditional working-class food from the East End of London. It consists of a minced beef pie and mashed potato that's then covered in a thin parsley sauce called liquor. Pie and mash shops can still be found across the city.
'I always get pie and mash before going to the football.'

'piece of cake'

piece of cake (idiom)
if something is a piece of cake, it is easy to do.
'Learning how to drive was a piece of cake.'

piggy in the middle (phrase)
a game usually played by children in which two people throw a ball to each other and try to make sure a person in between them doesn't get it.
'One of my favourite games to play with my little cousins is piggy in the middle.'

pillock (noun) /ˈpɪlək/ rude
another word for 'idiot'.
'Wasim is such a pillock. He left the car lights on all night and now the battery is dead.'

pinch (verb) /pɪntʃ/
to steal something.
'Have you pinched my lighter?'

pint (noun) /paɪnt/
a measurement of alcohol (568 ml).
'I'll have a pint of lager, please.'

pish (noun) /pɪʃ/ rude
a Scottish word for 'urine'.
'I need to run home – I need a pish.'

pish (adjective) /pɪʃ/ rude
a Scottish term meaning 'not very good' or 'rubbish'.
'That was another pish performance from Scotland.'

piss about/around (phrasal verb) /pɪs əˈbaʊt/ rude
to waste time doing unimportant things.
A – 'Did you write your essay?'
B – 'No! I've just been pissing around all day avoiding it.'

piss artist (noun) /ˈpɪs ɑːtɪst/ rude
someone who behaves incompetently or pretends to have skills or knowledge they don't really have.
'That joiner was a total piss artist – he did a really poor job and charged us a fortune for it.'

piss (it) down (with rain) (phrasal verb) /ˈpɪs daʊn/ rude
a slang term meaning to rain heavily.
'We'll need to take an umbrella, it's pissing it down out there.'

pissed (adjective) /pɪst/ rude
in British English, it's a slang word for 'drunk'. In American English, it means 'angry'.
'I've never seen my uncle as pissed as last night.'

pissed off (adjective) /pɪst ˈɒf/ rude
a slang term for 'angry'.
'Haruki is really pissed off we forgot his birthday.'

pisshead (noun) /ˈpɪshed/ rude
someone who drinks a very large amount of alcohol on a regular basis.
'In my student days, I was a complete pisshead.'

piss off (phrasal verb) /ˈpɪs ɒf/ rude
a rude way to say ‘go away’.
‘I’m sick of you moaning about everything. Piss off and leave me alone.’

piss (somebody) off (phrasal verb) /ˈpɪs ɒf/ rude
to make someone annoyed or angry.
‘He never texts me back. It’s really starting to piss me off.’

piss-take (noun) /ˈpɪs teɪk/ rude
the act of making fun of or teasing someone.
‘Don’t take what I said so seriously. It was just a piss-take.’

piss-up (noun) /ˈpɪs ʌp/ rude
a slang term for an occasion when a group of people get together to drink lots of alcohol.
‘Let’s have a piss-up to celebrate Will’s birthday.’

piss yourself (laughing) (phrase) rude
to laugh a lot.
‘We all pissed ourselves when Sven slipped over on the dance floor and ended up flat on his face.’

play up (phrasal verb) /pleɪ ˈʌp/
if someone plays up, they behave badly. If something plays up, it stops working properly.
‘My wifi is playing up so I’m going to work in the cafe downstairs.’

plonk (noun) /plɒŋk/ slang
cheap wine.
‘Shall we get a bottle of plonk to have with our meal?’

plonk (verb) /plɒŋk/
to put something down on a surface carelessly or heavily.
‘Don’t just plonk your chair there, we can’t see the TV.’

plonker (noun) /ˈplɒŋkə/ rude
a synonym of ‘idiot’.
‘I’m such a plonker! I’ve left my keys at the office.’

PMQs (noun) /piː em ˈkjuːz/
abbreviation of ‘Prime Minister’s Questions’, which is a session in the House of Commons every week when MPs can ask the Prime Minister questions.
‘I love watching PMQs and seeing how the Prime Minister deals with tough questions.’

polling station (noun) /ˈpəʊlɪŋ steɪʃən/
the place where people go to vote in an election.
‘The nearest polling station is about a mile away.’

Pompey (noun) /ˈpɒmpi/
an informal name for ‘Portsmouth’.
‘I’m a Pompey girl, born and bred.’

‘A “pony” is just one example of a slang term used in British English for money. Others include a “monkey”, a “quid” and “shrapnel”.’

Teacher Tom

pony (noun) /ˈpəʊni/ slang
London slang for £25.
'Can I borrow a pony to buy Grandma a birthday present?'

pootle (verb) /ˈpu:təl/
to move in a leisurely and relaxed way or do things that you enjoy but aren't essential.
'I think we're just going to pootle around town for a bit before heading home.'

pop (verb) /pɒp/
to go somewhere for a short time and return. It is often used with a preposition.
'I'm just going to pop out for a minute to get some fresh air.'

pop (noun) /pɒp/ slang
a carbonated drink.
'Would you kids like a bottle of pop for the journey home?'

poppycock (noun) /ˈpɒpikɒk/
an old-fashioned way to say that something is nonsense.
'This new housing bill the government has announced is absolute poppycock.'

pop your clogs (idiom)
a euphemistic phrase meaning 'to die'.
'Our hamster popped his clogs last weekend and the kids are devastated.'

pork pie (noun) /pɔ:k ˈpaɪ/
a type of meat pie made from chopped pork with bits of jelly encased in pastry. It's commonly eaten on picnics or as a snack.
'I've baked a bunch of pork pies for our picnic.'

porridge (noun) /ˈpɒrɪdʒ/
a grain (often oats) simmered in milk or water, eaten for breakfast. In Scotland, people traditionally cooked it with salt, whereas that isn't the case elsewhere. These days there is a wide variety of things you can add, such as sugar, honey, fresh fruit, seeds, etc.
'In the winter, there's no better way to start the day than with a bowl of porridge.'

porridge (noun) /ˈpɒrɪdʒ/ slang
an old-fashioned word for a prison sentence.
'My grandad did porridge at Wormwood Scrubs prison in west London.'

posh (adjective) /pɒʃ/
classy or sophisticated.
'We went to that new posh restaurant that has just opened on Park Street.'

posho (noun) /ˈpɒʃəʊ/
a posh person you find annoying.
'He's friends with a bunch of poshos from Surrey.'

postcode lottery (noun) /pəʊstkəʊd ˈlɒtəri/
the unfortunate situation in which people are able to get different levels of medical treatment and health services depending on which area of Britain they live.
'It's a disgrace that Jihyun can't get adequate health services just because of where he lives. It's just another example of the postcode lottery.'

postgraduate (noun) /pəʊstˈgrædʒuət/
someone studying for a further qualification having received their degree (also 'postgrad').
'The postgraduates on my course are mostly in their 30s with families and kids.'

‘it’s proper miserable outside’

potter (verb) /ˈpɒtə/
to occupy yourself in a pleasant way by doing small tasks or activities, usually around your home.
‘I always like to have one weekend day at home to potter about doing bits and bobs.’

poxy (adjective) /ˈpɒksi/
of little value or importance.
‘Do you know what he gave me for my birthday? This poxy mug and a pair of socks.’

prat (noun) /præt/ rude
someone you believe to be stupid or foolish.
‘You look an absolute prat in that striped shirt!’

prefect (noun) /ˈpriːfekt/
a senior pupil in secondary school who has extra duties and responsibilities.
‘I really wanted to be a prefect at school just so I could boss my friends about.’

preggers (adjective) /ˈpregəz/ slang
pregnant.
‘Have you heard Sophie is preggers?’

premium bond (noun) /ˈpriːmiəm ˈbɒnd/
a government-run lottery. You can buy a ticket and draws are made monthly.
‘My aunt bought me some premium bonds when I was a child.’

prep school (noun) /ˈprep skuːl/
a private school for children aged 7–13 (short for ‘preparatory’).
‘Our sons go to a prep school in Hampstead.’

prezzie (noun) /ˈprezi/ slang
alternative form of ‘present’.
‘We need to buy your nan a birthday prezzie.’

private school (noun) /ˈpraɪvət skuːl/
a school that is not government-funded and requires parents to pay a fee every term.
‘I’d love my kids to go to private school but we simply can’t afford it.’

proper (adverb) /ˈprɒpə/ slang
a word used to emphasise something, similar to ‘extremely’.
‘It’s proper miserable outside, let’s stay in and watch a film.’

prop (up) the bar (phrase)
to stand at the bar of a pub and drink (also ‘prop the bar’).
‘There aren’t any seats so let’s just prop up the bar.’

PTA (noun) /piː tiː ˈeɪ/
parent-teacher association. An organisation of parents and teachers who meet in order to think of ideas to help improve the school.
‘The PTA meets once a month.’

pub (noun) /pʌb/
short for 'public house'. A building in which alcohol is sold and consumed.
'There are so many great pubs in Greenwich.'

pub crawl (noun) /ˈpʌb krɔːl/
a visit to numerous pubs, one after the other, and having at least one drink in each.
'There's a pub crawl tonight at the university if you fancy coming?'

public school (noun) /ˈpʌblɪk skuːl/
an elite group of British private schools which students pay very high fees to attend. The most famous examples of public schools are Eton and Harrow.
'It's no surprise that many of our Prime Ministers have gone to public school.'

pudding (noun) /ˈpʊdɪŋ/
a sweet dish served at the end of a meal. It's a synonym of 'dessert' (short form is 'pud').
'What's for pudding, Dad?'

pukka (adjective) /ˈpʌkə/ slang
very good.
'These mince pies are pukka, Mrs Williams. Can I have the recipe?'

pull (verb) /pʊl/ slang
to succeed in having sexual relations with someone.
'Did you pull anyone last night?'

pull a sickie (phrase) slang
to take the day off work or school by pretending you are ill, even though you are perfectly healthy.
'I've never pulled a sickie in my life.'

pumps (noun) /pʌmps/
a casual soft shoe used for sports and activities (mainly in the Midlands, the north of England and Scotland).
'Mum have you seen my pumps? I left them on the doorstep last night and now I can't find them.'

Punch and Judy show (noun) /pʌntʃ ən ˈdʒuːdi ʃəʊ/
a puppet show that is traditional British seaside entertainment for children.
'We used to go and watch the Punch and Judy show every week when we were kids.'

punnet (noun) /ˈpʌnɪt/
a small container that holds fruit.
'Can you pick up a punnet of strawberries from the supermarket, please?'

punter (noun) /ˈpʌntə/
a customer or user of services, particularly a customer of betting shops.
'Theme parks are reducing their prices to get more punters through the door.'

purple patch (phrase)
a period of time when a person or team is successful or lucky (usually in sports).
'Spurs are having a bit of a purple patch right now with five wins in a row.'

Q

quango (noun) /ˈkwæŋgəʊ/
a quasi-autonomous non-governmental UK organisation started by the government but not run by them.
'The British Council is a quango that promotes British interests around the world.'

Queen's English (noun) /kwi:nz ˈɪŋglɪʃ/
the pronunciation of the royals and upper classes in Britain (also 'King's English').
'The only time I ever hear the Queen's English is when I watch "The Crown" on Netflix.'

queue (noun) /kju:/
a line of people or vehicles waiting for something.
'There is always a massive queue to get into the Wimbledon tennis championships.'

queue (verb) /kju:/
to wait in a line of people or vehicles.
'I've been queuing at the post office for over an hour.'

queue-jumping (noun) /ˈkju: dʒʌmpɪŋ/
the act of someone unfairly moving ahead in a queue.
'If there's one thing I hate, it's queue-jumping!'

quid (noun) /kwɪd/ slang
one pound sterling.
'Can I borrow a quid for the bus?'

'can I borrow a quid?'

R

radge (noun) /rædʒ/ slang
someone acting in an angry or wild manner (used in the east of Scotland and the northeast of England).
'There was a radge on the bus making all kinds of bother for the driver.'

radge (adjective) /rædʒ/ slang
angry, wild or crazy (used in the east of Scotland and the northeast of England).
'She seems a little bit radge, did you say anything to upset her?'

RAF (noun) /ɑː eɪ ˈef/
Royal Air Force. The air force of the United Kingdom.
'Our son is thinking of joining the RAF when he leaves school.'

rah (noun) /rɑː/ slang
a very posh person.
'There were so many rahs at Bristol Uni.'

rank (adjective) /ræŋk/ slang
disgusting.
'The food at that place is rank! Let's go somewhere else.'

rather! (exclamation) /rɑːˈðə/
an old-fashioned way to say 'yes'.
A – 'Do you think we should host a New Year's Eve party this year?'
B – 'Rather!'

ratty (adjective) /ˈræti/
becoming annoyed quickly.
'Jen's husband gets a bit ratty when he hasn't eaten.'

read (verb) /riːd/
to study a subject, usually at university.
'She went to Edinburgh to read English and Politics.'

readies (noun) /ˈrediːz/ slang
cash.
'Have you got any readies I can use to pay the builders?'

recce (noun) /ˈreki/
short for 'reconnaissance'. The act of gathering information about something.
'When I worked in TV we used to do recces for potential filming locations all the time.'

Received Pronunciation (noun) /rɪsiːvd prənʌnsiˈeɪʃən/
a British English accent associated with the educated and wealthy. It has no geographical root but it is commonly found in London and the south of England (abbreviation 'RP').
'In Received Pronunciation, it's very important to pronounce every sound as clearly as possible.'

reception (noun) /rɪˈsepʃən/
the first year of infant school for children aged 4–5 in England and Wales.
'Mrs Bakewell is teaching reception next term.'

reckon (verb) /ˈrekən/
a synonym of 'think'.
'My girlfriend reckons I should get a haircut.'

‘what do you reckon?’

red-brick (noun) /ˈred brɪk/
any of the British universities that were built in the industrial cities such as Liverpool and Birmingham around the late 19th and early 20th centuries. They derive their name from the gothic architecture of the buildings.
‘My teachers are really encouraging me to apply to one of the red-bricks to read history.’

red-brick (adjective) /ˈred brɪk/
used to describe a collection of British universities that were built in industrial cities like Liverpool and Birmingham.
‘Have you applied to any of the red-brick universities, Anna?’

redundant (adjective) /rɪˈdʌndənt/
unemployed because your employer no longer needs you.
‘They’ve made 100 people redundant this week in the hope of cutting costs.’

remembrance poppy (noun) /rɪˈmembrəns pɒpi/
the red poppy that people wear in the first weeks of November as a way to remember and acknowledge the sacrifice made by people in the British and Commonwealth military who died for their country.
‘I lost my remembrance poppy somewhere on the Tube while rushing to meet you.’

return (ticket) (noun) /rɪˈtɜːn tɪkɪt/
a travel ticket from one place to another and then back again.
‘I’d like a return to St Albans, please.’

revise (verb) /rɪˈvaɪz/
to reread work that you have already studied in preparation for an exam or test.
‘Harry’s coming round to revise for our maths exam.’

rib (someone) (verb) /rɪb/
to tease someone.
‘My mates used to rib me because I would always blush when I talked to girls.’

right (adjective) /raɪt/
used as an intensifier in a similar way to ‘absolute’.
‘You were a right troublemaker when you were at school.’

ring (verb) /rɪŋ/
to call or phone someone.
‘Your sister rang for you but she didn’t leave a message.’

rollicking (noun) /ˈrɒlɪkɪŋ/
a very strong telling off or reprimand.
‘We got an absolute rollicking from the headteacher for letting off the school fire extinguisher.’

ropey (adjective) /ˈrəʊpi/
poor quality, inadequate.
'The connection's a bit ropey, Sam – can you check your wifi?'

ropey (adjective) /ˈrəʊpi/
not feeling very well.
'Are you OK, Marina? You look a bit ropey.'

rota (noun) /ˈrəʊtə/
a list with the order in which different people have to do a particular job, e.g. waiters and waitresses in a restaurant.
'I'll send out July's rota tomorrow.'

round (noun) /raʊnd/
a set of drinks bought for a group of people, usually within a system. Each person takes it in turn to buy a round for everyone else.
'What do you want guys? It's my round.'

roundabout (noun) /ˈraʊndəbaʊt/
a circular area where three or more roads meet. A car goes around the roundabout until it reaches the road it requires.
'When I was learning how to drive, I hated going near roundabouts.'

row (noun) /raʊ/
a loud argument.
'My boyfriend and I broke up because we found ourselves rowing about every little thing.'

row (verb) /raʊ/
to argue in a loud manner.
'The couple next door have been rowing all evening.'

Royal Mail (noun) /rɔɪəl ˈmeɪl/
a postal service in the United Kingdom.
'I sent your birthday card via Royal Mail.'

rubbish (adjective) /ˈrʌbɪʃ/ slang
not very good.
'This book is absolutely rubbish, don't waste your time reading it.'

rucksack (noun) /ˈrʌksæk/
a bag with straps that you wear on two shoulders.
'Would you like to get a new rucksack before school starts?'

rugger (noun) /ˈrʌgə/
an informal term for 'rugby'.
'I think the BBC are showing the rugger this afternoon.'

rumpy-pumpy (noun) /rʌmpɪ ˈpʌmpi/ rude
an old-fashioned, humorous way to refer to sexual intercourse.
'This film isn't really suitable for kids. There's a bit of rumpy-pumpy at the beginning.'

'you look a bit ropey'

S

sack off (phrasal verb) /sæk ˈɒf/ slang
if you sack something off, you avoid or stop doing it.
'I know we had plans to go out tonight, but can we just sack them off and stay in?'

saddo (noun) /ˈsædəʊ/
an insulting term for a socially inadequate person similar to a 'loser'.
A – 'Only saddos play computer games.'
B – 'What are you talking about? It's super cool these days.'

samey (adjective) /ˈseɪmi/
boring because there is no variety.
'I don't really like their new album, the songs are all so samey.'

Sandringham (noun) /ˈsændrɪŋəm/
a residence in Norfolk, owned by the King.
'The royal family spent the weekend at Sandringham.'

sarky (adjective) /ˈsɑːki/
another way to say 'sarcastic'.
'I can't help making sarky comments at work, I'm going to get myself into trouble one of these days.'

sarnie (noun) /ˈsɑːni/
another way to say 'sandwich'.
'I really fancy a sarnie for lunch.'

SAS (noun) /es eɪ ˈes/
abbreviation for 'Special Air Service', which is an elite military force in the British army that conducts highly dangerous secretive missions.
'I signed up to an SAS training camp and didn't survive the first day.'

scally (noun) /ˈskɒli/ rude
an offensive slang word for a young, boisterous, often uneducated, boy or girl.
'There is a bunch of scallies hanging outside our house smoking, drinking and causing a lot of noise.'

scarper (verb) /ˈskɑːpə/
to leave or escape very quickly.
'By the time the police had got there, the thieves had scarpered.'

school run (noun) /ˈskuːl rʌn/
the journey parents make when they take their children to school and bring them back home.
'I'm going to leave home early tomorrow so I can avoid the traffic from the school run.'

scone (noun) /skɒn/ or /skəʊn/
a small, lightly sweetened cake that's served as part of an afternoon tea. The pronunciation of this word is a hotly debated topic; I'll let you decide which one to use.
'Auntie Susie's freshly baked scones are to die for!'

Scotch egg (noun) /skɒtʃˈeg/
a classic picnic food that also makes a great snack. It's a boiled egg wrapped in pork meat then covered in breadcrumbs and deep-fried.
'I bought a few Scotch eggs for our picnic tomorrow.'

Scouse (noun) /ˈskaʊs/
the accent and dialect found in and around the Liverpool area.
'My flatmate speaks with a thick Scouse accent.'

Scouser (noun) /ˈskaʊsə/
someone from Liverpool.
'I met a bunch of Scousers while travelling in Thailand last year.'

scran (noun) /skræn/ slang
a slang word for 'food', used mostly in northern dialects.
'Do you want some scran before you go out?'

scrap (noun) /skræp/ slang
a fight.
'When I was at school we used to have scraps with the school down the road all the time.'

scrap (verb) /skræp/ slang
to fight.
'As a kid, I was always scrapping with my little brother.'

screw (verb) /skru:/ rude
to have sex.
'Did you and Andy screw last night?'

screw (noun) /skru:/ slang
a term for a prison guard, usually used by inmates.
'My brother-in-law works as a screw in Belmarsh.'

scrub up well (idiom)
used to say that someone looks good and clearly made an effort to do so.
'I love seeing my sons in their suits. They do scrub up well.'

scruff (noun) /skrʌf/
someone who is untidy.
'Sam, you look like an absolute scruff. At least iron your shirt.'

scupper (verb) /ˈskʌpə/
to spoil or obstruct something, e.g. a plan or an opportunity.
'This ankle injury has scuppered my chances of running the London marathon.'

Secretary of State (noun) /sekrətəri əv ˈsteɪt/
a politician in charge of a particular government department, e.g. the Secretary of State for Health.
'They've just announced the new Secretary of State for Education.'

semi-detached house (noun) /ˈsemi dɪtætʃt haʊs/
a house which is connected to another house on just one side.
'In the suburbs of London, you'll see lots of semi-detached houses.'

send someone to Coventry (idiom)
a very old-fashioned phrase. If you send someone to Coventry, you refuse to speak to them as a way of punishing them.
'Why isn't Samantha talking to us? Maybe she's sent us to Coventry.'

senior citizen (noun) /si:njə ˈsɪtɪzən/
a term used to describe an older adult. You might also hear 'OAP' (short for 'old-age pensioner') but this isn't the preferred term anymore and is seen as old-fashioned.
'There's a coffee morning for senior citizens at the village hall tomorrow.'

shadow cabinet (noun) /ʃædəʊ ˈkæbɪnət/
the group of members of the opposition party who hold ministerial positions to mirror the government's cabinet of ministers.
'Another shadow cabinet minister has just resigned.'

shag (noun) /ʃæg/ rude
the act of having sex.
'I can't remember the last shag I had.'

shag (verb) /ʃæg/ rude
to have sex.
A – *'Did you sleep well?'*
B – *'No! There were people shagging really loudly in the room next door to me.'*

shambles (noun) /ˈʃæmbəlz/
if something is a shambles, it is badly organised and confusing.
'The office party was an absolute shambles! The organisers hadn't even booked a DJ!'

shambolic (adjective) /ʃæmˈbɒlɪk/
completely and utterly chaotic and disorganised.
'I enjoy working for this company but the way things are run is pretty shambolic.'

shandy (noun) /ˈʃændi/
an alcoholic drink of beer mixed with lemonade.
A – *'What can I get you? '*
B – *'I'll have a shandy, please.'*

sharpish (adverb) /ˈʃɑːpɪʃ/
an informal word for 'quickly'.
'We need to leave sharpish, otherwise we'll be late for class.'

shattered (adjective) /ˈʃætəd/
very tired.
'The kids are shattered, let's put them straight to bed.'

shedload (noun) /ˈʃedləʊd/
a large amount of something.
'Don't bring any food, I've got a shedload in my fridge left over from last night.'

shell out (phrasal verb) /ʃel ˈaʊt/
to spend a lot of money on something.
'Dad's just shelled out a grand on a brand-new TV for the living room.'

shepherd's pie (noun) /ʃepədz ˈpaɪ/
a dish of minced lamb topped with mashed potato and cooked in the oven.
'I found a really good recipe for shepherd's pie on TikTok.'

shipping forecast (noun) /ˈʃɪpɪŋ fɔːkɑːst/
a radio programme broadcast on the BBC that describes the weather at sea around the United Kingdom.
'There's something really reassuring about listening to the shipping forecast when you are in bed.'

shire (noun) /ʃaɪə/
a county in England or Wales, e.g. Yorkshire or Leicestershire. It's often used to describe rural areas of natural beauty that contrast with built-up urban areas. (also 'the shires').
'You should definitely try and explore some of the shires while you are in England.'

shirty (adjective) /ˈʃɜːti/
an informal word for 'bad-tempered'.
'There's no need to get shirty, I'll do the dishes when I get back.'

shite (adjective) /ʃaɪt/ rude
an alternative to 'shit'.
'It looks like the weather is going to be shite for the next few days.'

shit-stirrer (noun) /ˈʃɪt stɜːrə/ rude
an offensive term for someone who causes trouble deliberately, usually by passing on information that is secret or untrue.
'I never said I didn't like my new flatmates! Don't be such a shit-stirrer.'

shout (noun) /ʃaʊt/
an informal word meaning someone's turn to buy a round of drinks or dinner.
'What do you guys want to drink? It's my shout!'

short-arse (noun) /ˈʃɔːt ɑːs/ rude
a rude word to call someone 'short'.
A – 'How come you are so tall? Are your parents tall as well?'
B – 'No, my dad is a short-arse.'

shrapnel (noun) /ˈʃræpnəl/
an informal word for loose change, i.e. coins.
'Have you got any shrapnel I can borrow to put in the parking meter?'

shut your trap/gob/mouth (phrase)
an informal, aggressive way to tell someone to stop talking.
A – 'Charlie's team are going to thrash you guys tonight.'
B – 'Shut your gob! They haven't got a chance against us.'

skew-whiff (adjective) /skjuː ˈwɪf/
describes something that is not straight.
'That painting is hanging a little skew-whiff, don't you think?'

skint (adjective) /skɪnt/ slang
having no money.
'When is payday? I'm absolutely skint!'

skive off (from something) (phrasal verb) /skaɪv ˈɒf/ slang
to not attend school or work, without a good reason.
'We used to skive off from school all the time.'

silly billy (noun) /ˈsɪli bɪli/
someone who behaves in a silly way.
'Oh Manu, you are a silly billy!'

simples! (exclamation) /ˈsɪmpəlz/
used after a statement that has given the solution to a problem. It comes from a TV advert featuring a Russian meerkat.
'Mate, if you want to lose weight, you've got to go to the gym more often. Simples!'

(the) Six Nations (noun) /sɪks ˈneɪʃənz/
an international rugby tournament between England, Scotland, Wales, Ireland, France and Italy, played every spring.
'The Six Nations is kicking off this weekend with Scotland vs England.'

slag (someone) off (phrasal verb) /slæg ˈɒf/ slang
to criticise someone in a mean way.
'Why are you slagging off Misha behind her back?'

'I'm skint!'

slanging match (noun) /ˈslæŋɪŋ mætʃ/ slang
an argument between two sides in which they exchange angry insults (also 'slagging match').
'My sister and I had a huge slanging match on Saturday night after she'd said my boyfriend wasn't invited to her birthday party.'

'slap and tickle'

slap and tickle (noun) /slæp ən ˈtɪkəl/ rude
a humorous, slightly old-fashioned term for kissing, cuddling and sexual activity.
'We went back to her place after the club for a bit of slap and tickle.'

slap-bang (adverb) /ˈslæp bæŋ/
exactly in a particular place.
'Trafalgar Square is slap-bang in the middle of London.'

slash (noun) /slæʃ/ rude
the act of urinating.
'Thiago's just having a slash and then we can go.'

sling your hook (phrase) slang
used to tell someone to leave.
'After their big argument, Priya told Ash to sling his hook.'

slip road (noun) /ˈslɪp rəʊd/
a road that allows drivers to get on or off a motorway.
'Remember to slow down when you turn off at the slip road.'

Sloane Ranger (noun) /sləʊn ˈreɪndʒə/
a derogatory term used to describe the stereotypical young upper-class woman from west London. There is an area in Chelsea called Sloane Square and the people who live there are generally extremely wealthy (also 'Sloanie').
'I saw so many Sloane Rangers on the King's Road this morning.'

small print (noun) /ˈsmɔːl prɪnt/
the text in formal agreements that is written in very small font. It usually holds important information.
'You have to check the small print before signing a contract.'

smoggie (noun) /ˈsmɒgi/
a nickname for someone from Teeside in northeast England and for the local accent.
'All my brother-in-law's family are smoggies.'

snaffle (verb) /ˈsnæfəl/
to quickly take something without asking, usually something that isn't yours.
'Who has snaffled all the biscuits?'

snap (noun) /snæp/
an informal word for a photograph.
'I loved all your holiday snaps from your trip to Thailand.'

snog (noun) /snɒg/ slang
a passionate kiss that lasts for a period of time.
'Did you manage to get a snog last night?'

snog (verb) /snɒg/ slang
to kiss someone in a passionate way for a period of time.
'I snogged one of my colleagues at the staff Christmas party!'

SNP (noun) /es en ˈpiː/
an abbreviation for the 'Scottish National Party', which is a political party in Scotland.
'The SNP have done better than expected in the local elections.'

so-and-so (noun) /ˈsəʊ ən səʊ/
a person who is considered to have a negative characteristic.
'My neighbour is a nosy old so-and-so.'

soap dodger (noun) /ˈsəʊp dɒdʒə/ rude
a derogatory term for someone who is unclean or doesn't wash.
'Our last housemate was a bit of a soap dodger, so we'd like someone with good hygiene next time.'

sod (noun) /sɒd/ rude
a light-hearted, informal word for a person.
'I can't believe you got an upgrade – you lucky sod!'

sod all (phrase) slang
a slightly rude phrase meaning 'nothing'.
'I've done sod all today!'

sod it/that (exclamation) /ˈsɒd ɪt/ slang
a slightly rude way to show anger or annoyance at something or someone.
'Ah sod it! Let's give up trying to build this wardrobe for today.'

sod off (exclamation) /ˈsɒd ɒf/ rude
a rude way to tell someone to go away.
'Sod off and leave me alone! I've had enough of you moaning for one day.'

solicitor (noun) /səˈlɪsɪtə/
a British lawyer who gives legal advice.
'I've hired a solicitor to help me with the selling of my house.'

soppy (adjective) /ˈsɒpi/
overly emotional and romantic in a way that seems silly or embarrassing.
'Pepe wrote me a really soppy note saying how much he missed me.'

sorted (adjective) /ˈsɔːtɪd/
an informal word for 'organised' or 'arranged'.
A – 'Do you need anything from the shop?'
B – 'No, I'm sorted, thanks.'

Sorted! (exclamation) /ˈsɔːtɪd/ slang
a slang term used mainly in the north of England to mean 'OK' or 'great'.
A – 'I just passed my driving theory test!'
B – 'Sorted, mate!'

sound (adjective) /saʊnd/
good or nice.
'My new colleagues seem really sound.'

Southerner (noun) /ˈsʌðənə/
someone from the south of England.
'Most of the people at my uni were Southerners.'

sozzled (adjective) /ˈsɒzəld/ slang
very drunk.
'I was completely sozzled after one glass of wine.'

spag bol (noun) /spæg ˈbɒl/
a shortened form of 'spaghetti bolognese'.
'I'm making spag bol for tea if you want some.'

'you're spot on!'

spanner in the works (idiom)
something that stops or spoils a plan or process.
'The rain has put a real spanner in the works for our picnic.'

spark out (adjective) /spɑ:k ˈaʊt/ slang
completely unconscious.
'Mate, Anthony Joshua would knock you spark out if you tried to box him.'

sparky (noun) /ˈspɑ:ki/ slang
an electrician.
'My son is training to be a sparky just like his dad.'

spend a penny (idiom)
an old-fashioned phrase meaning to go to the toilet.
'I'm just going to spend a penny before we leave.'

spenny (adjective) /ˈspeni/ slang
expensive.
'I'd love to come visit you but flights are a bit spenny at the moment.'

spiffing (adjective) /ˈspɪfɪŋ/
a very old-fashioned term for 'excellent'.
'Oh George, thank you for hosting last night's party. It was a spiffing occasion.'

splash out (on something) (phrasal verb) /splæʃ ˈaʊt/
to spend a lot of money on something.
'Let's splash out and book a fancy hotel for our anniversary.'

spod (noun) /spɒd/
a geeky person who studies a lot and isn't fashionable.
'My data science class is full of spods like me, I love it!'

Spoons (noun) /spu:nz/
the short form of 'Wetherspoons', a well-known pub chain in the UK.
'I'm having my leaving do at the Spoons in town.'

spot on (adjective) /spɒt ˈɒn/
exactly correct.
A – 'I reckon a house around here costs about £350,000. Am I right?'
B – 'You're spot on!'

spots (noun) /spɒts/
raised red marks on the skin, commonly found on teenagers.
'I had terrible spots growing up and I still get the odd spot on my forehead.'

sprog (noun) /sprɒg/ slang
a child.
'They've had four sprogs in five years.'

spud (noun) /spʌd/ slang
a potato.
'Would you like some spuds with your roast chicken?'

squaddie (noun) /ˈskwɒdi/ slang
a low-ranking soldier in the British army.
'You see a lot of squaddies in Chelmsford because there is an army barracks nearby.'

squidgy (adjective) /ˈskwɪdʒi/
soft and changing shape easily.
'I've bought Eliza a squidgy toy to play with.'

squire (noun) /skwaɪə/
an old-fashioned way to address a man, usually one of higher social standing.
'Good morning squire, can I help you with your bags?'

(the) squits (noun) /skwɪts/ rude
a slang term for 'diarrhoea'.
'I've had the squits all weekend. It's been miserable.'

stag do/party (noun) /ˈstæg duː/
the celebration a man has before he gets married.
'I said I wouldn't have a stag do but then my friends organised one anyway!'

'stag party'

stamp duty (noun) /ˈstæmp djuːti/
a type of tax you pay in England and Northern Ireland when you buy a property or piece of land.
'Don't forget, you've got to pay stamp duty on top of the amount they are asking for.'

St Andrew's Day (noun) /seɪnt ˈændruːz deɪ/
the day for St Andrew, the patron saint of Scotland.
'Every St Andrew's Day we have a ceilidh in the town hall.'

starkers (adjective) /ˈstɑːkəz/ slang
an informal, humorous word for 'naked'.
'My mother-in-law walked into our room without knocking and my wife and I were completely starkers.'

state school (noun) /ˈsteɪt skuːl/
a school that is funded by the government and therefore free to attend for all children.
'The vast majority of children in the UK go to a state school.'

St David's Day (noun) /seɪnt ˈdeɪvɪdz deɪ/
the day for St David, the patron saint of Wales.
'It's common for my family to celebrate St David's Day by picking daffodils in the woods.'

steady on (phrase)
an expression used to tell someone to be more reasonable or modify what they have just said.
A – 'That's it! Didier is going to have to move out. I'm sick and tired of his behaviour.'
B – 'Steady on! Let's have a chat about it with him first.'

steam in (phrasal verb) /stiːm ˈɪn/
to join or start a fight.
'I know you are angry but don't go steaming in! Just take a breath and try to calm down.'

St George's Day (noun) /seɪnt ˈdʒɔːdʒɪz deɪ/
the day for St George, the patron saint of England.
'England released a brand-new home kit on St George's Day.'

stick (noun) /stɪk/ slang
abuse or criticism.
'The England rugby team received a lot of stick after losing their fifth consecutive game.'

stitch (someone) up (phrasal verb) /stɪtʃ ˈʌp/ slang
to deliberately make sure someone gets the wrongful blame for something.
'I remember getting stitched up at school by a kid called Max who said I'd stolen his football boots.'

stodgy (adjective) /ˈstɒdʒi/
a word used to describe food that is heavy and filling.
'I had this beef pie for lunch that was so stodgy I couldn't finish it.'

stonker (noun) /ˈstɒŋkə/ slang
an informal term for something very big.
'I've baked her a stonker of a birthday cake.'

stonking (adjective) /ˈstɒŋkɪŋ/ slang
an informal word for 'very big' or 'very impressive'.
'Blimey Maggie! That's a stonking great garden you've got.'

St Patrick's Day (noun) /seɪnt ˈpætrɪks deɪ/
the day for St Patrick, the patron saint of Ireland.
'It isn't St Patrick's Day unless I've had a pint of Guinness.'

stramash (noun) /strəˈmaʃ/
a Scottish word meaning 'a noisy disagreement or brawl'.
'There was a huge stramash outside the pub last night.'

strop (noun) /strɒp/
a bad mood, usually because you have to do something you don't want to do.
'Connor had a strop because I wouldn't let him borrow my car.'

stroppy (adjective) /ˈstrɒpi/
moody and unpleasant.
'Were you a bit of a stroppy teenager?'

stuffed (adjective) /stʌft/
an informal way to say you are very full after eating a lot.
'That Sunday roast was delicious guys, I'm absolutely stuffed.'

subway (noun) /ˈsʌbweɪ/
an underground walkway (also 'underpass').
'Let's take the subway instead of trying to cross the busy road.'

summat (pronoun) /ˈsʌmət/
an informal variation of 'something', mainly used in the north of England.
'Do you want to do summat this weekend?'

Sunday roast (noun) /sʌndeɪ ˈrəʊst/
a quintessentially British meal consisting of roast meat, cooked vegetables and gravy.
'My grandma's Sunday roast is the best in the world.'

‘it’s swings and roundabouts’

sunshine (noun) /ˈsʌnʃaɪn/
an informal term of address for someone, usually affectionate.
‘Alright sunshine, are you ready to go?’

suss (something/someone) out
(phrasal verb) /sʌs ˈaʊt/
to discover or find out the things you need to know about something or someone.
‘We finally sussed out why Kiara has been so distant lately.’

sweet FA (phrase) rude
a phrase that means ‘absolutely nothing’. The FA stands for ‘fuck all’ and this phrase is used to avoid saying it.
‘I’ve heard sweet FA from the recruitment agency about my job interview.’

sweet Fanny Adams (phrase) rude
a slightly rude phrase that means ‘absolutely nothing’. It’s used as a way to avoid saying ‘fuck all’, which is seen as much ruder.
‘I won sweet Fanny Adams at the horse races today.’

swings and roundabouts (idiom)
used to talk about a situation that will even itself out in the end, i.e. the positives will balance out the negatives.
‘If we can’t get a flight tonight, we can always catch one tomorrow. It’s more expensive but we get an extra night in the city, so it’s swings and roundabouts.’

swot (noun) /swɒt/
a slightly mean term for someone (usually a child) who studies very hard.
‘All the kids at school called me a swot because I did extra homework.’

T

ta! (interjection) /tɑː/
an informal way to say 'thank you'.
A – 'Here's your tea, Mum.'
B – 'Ta love!'

tad (noun) /tæd/
a small amount.
'It's a tad cold in here, don't you think?'

tailback (noun) /ˈteɪlbæk/
a long line of traffic that moves very slowly or not at all.
'There are tailbacks all along the North Circular tonight after an accident.'

take a piss (phrase) rude
to urinate.
'Is there anywhere around here I can take a piss?'

take a pop (at someone) (phrase)
to criticise someone.
'Did you hear the Brighton manager take a pop at the FA for postponing their match?'

take a punt (on something) (phrase)
slang
to have a speculative go at something that involves risk, e.g. gambling or investment.
'I took a punt on Wales winning the World Cup and they were knocked out in the first round.'

take the piss (out of someone) (phrase)
rude
a very informal phrase meaning to tease or mock someone (also 'take the mickey').
'My mates take the piss out of me because I still can't ride a bike.'

tally-ho (exclamation) /tæli ˈhəʊ/
traditionally used in hunting to announce the sighting of a fox. It can also be used to say goodbye in a humorous, old-fashioned way.
'Tally-ho chaps, I'm off to bed.'

ta-ra (exclamation) /tə ˈrɑː/
a way of saying 'goodbye', used mostly in the north of England.
'Ta-ra kids, I'll see you tonight after school.'

'don't take the piss!'

ta-ra a bit (exclamation) /tə rɑː ə ˈbɪt/
an informal way to say 'goodbye', mainly used in the Midlands.
'I'm off to the Bullring, ta-ra a bit.'

tart (oneself) up (phrasal verb) /tɑːt ˈʌp/
an informal phrase meaning to make yourself more attractive with makeup, clothes, jewellery, etc.
A – 'Where's Amy?'
B – 'She's in the loo tarting herself up.'

Tartan Army (noun) /tɑːtən ˈɑːmi/
the name given to the group of fans who follow the Scottish football team.
'The Tartan Army celebrated their victory over England in Trafalgar Square.'

tear-up (noun) /ˈteə ʌp/ slang
an informal word for a fight.
'Two of the lads had a bit of a tear-up during the match.'

tekkers (noun) /ˈtekəz/ slang
used in a sporting context to mean a high level of skill. It's a shortened form of 'technique'.
'Stan's got the best tekkers in the team.'

telly (noun) /ˈteli/
short for 'television'.
'There's nothing good on the telly tonight.'

ten a penny (phrase)
very common (also 'two a penny').
'Around Shoreditch, trendy coffee shops are ten a penny.'

'ten a penny'

tat (noun) /tæt/
items that are in poor condition or of very low quality.
'Most of the shops around Leicester Square sell tourist tat.'

tea (noun) /tiː/
used mainly in the north of England as the word for the evening meal.
'Mam, can Mohammed come round for tea tonight?'

Team GB (noun) /tiːm dʒiː ˈbiː/
the Great Britain and Northern Ireland Olympic team.
'Her dream is to compete for Team GB at the Olympics.'

tenner (noun) /ˈtenə/ slang
ten pounds sterling.
A – 'How much is it to get in?'
B – 'Tickets are a tenner.'

terraced house (noun) /terəst ˈhaʊs/
a house connected to houses on both sides.
'We're hoping to buy one of those cute terraced houses near Columbia Road Flower Market.'

(the) Territorial Army (noun) /terɪtɔːriəl ˈɑːmi/
a voluntary reserve army force (now known as the Army Reserve).
'I joined the Territorial Army so that I could get basic army training and learn new skills.'

thou/thee (pronoun) /ðaʊ/ or /ðiː/
used in the Yorkshire dialect as a replacement for the second person singular.
'How are thee today, Hugo?'

tick (noun) /tɪk/
an informal term for a very short moment.
'I'll be there in a tick, just wait where you are.'

ticket tout (noun) /ˈtɪkɪt ˈtaʊt/
someone who makes their money by buying tickets and selling them on for a profit.
'There are always ticket touts standing outside the big concerts trying to sell tickets.'

tickety-boo (adjective) /tɪkɪti ˈbuː/
an old-fashioned way to say everything is as you want it to be.
A – 'How's your trip going?'
B – 'Tickety-boo, thanks.'

ticking off (noun) /tɪkɪŋ ˈɒf/
a light scolding or telling off.
'I just got a ticking off from my neighbour for parking in front of his drive.'

tick (someone) off (phrasal verb) /tɪk ˈɒf/
to criticise or scold someone for doing something wrong.
'The teacher ticked me off for chewing gum in her class.'

tight-arse (noun) /ˈtaɪt ɑːs/ rude
someone who is stingy and not willing to spend money.
'I can't believe you didn't leave a tip for the waiter! You're such a tight-arse.'

tipping it down (phrase)
raining heavily.
'Take your umbrella with you, it's absolutely tipping it down out there.'

tired and emotional (phrase)
a humorous phrase meaning 'drunk'.
'I'm going to take Felipe home, he's a little tired and emotional.'

tit (noun) /tɪt/ rude
a vulgar word for a woman's breast. Also used as an insult similar to 'idiot'.
'Do I look a bit of a tit in this hat?'

titchy (adjective) /ˈtɪtʃi/
very small.
'Oh my goodness! Your hamster is titchy! How old is she?'

toad-in-the-hole (noun) /təʊd ɪn ðə ˈhəʊl/
a classic British dish made of sausages encased in a giant Yorkshire pudding batter.
'My gran has promised to show me how to make her legendary toad-in-the-hole.'

todger (noun) /ˈtɒdʒə/ rude
a rude slang term for 'penis'.
'How many other words for penis other than todger can you think of?'

toe-rag (noun) /ˈtəʊ ræɡ/ slang
someone who behaves in a naughty or malicious way.
'That little toe-rag has stolen my bike!'

toff (noun) /tɒf/
a disapproving term for a posh or rich person.
'The TV show "Made in Chelsea" is full of toffs who love a bit of drama.'

(get) togged up/out (phrasal verb) /tɒgd ˈʌp/
to get dressed for a special occasion.
'All the lads got togged out for the rugby club Christmas party.'

Tom, Dick and Harry (noun) /tɒm dɪk ænd ˈhæri/
a phrase used to refer to ordinary people (also 'Tom, Dick or Harry').
'Darts isn't a sport! Any Tom, Dick or Harry could play it to a high level with enough training.'

tommy K (noun) /tɒmi ˈkeɪ/ slang
an informal variation of 'tomato ketchup'.
'Can you pass me the tommy K, please?'

(the) Toon (noun) /tuːn/
a nickname for Newcastle. Newcastle United fans are called the 'Toon Army'.
'There's no better place in the world than the Toon for a night out.'

top (oneself) (verb) /tɒp/ slang
to die by suicide.
'My friend threatened to top himself last night so we've called the authorities for help.'

top up (phrasal verb) /tɒp ˈʌp/
to add more money to an account, e.g. an oyster card or phone credit.
'Now you can use the app to top up your phone credit.'

top-up (noun) /ˈtɒp ʌp/
an extra amount of something to meet the necessary amount, e.g. money or liquid.
'Would you like a top-up on your wine Margot?'

Tory (noun) /ˈtɔːri/
someone who supports the Conservative Party.
'I live in a village with a lot of Tory supporters.'

tosh (noun) /tɒʃ/
an old-fashioned way to say 'nonsense'.
'I've never heard so much tosh in all my life.'

tosser (noun) /ˈtɒsə/ rude
a rude insult for someone you think is an idiot.
'I just saw this complete tosser throw his crisp packet on the floor.'

tosspot (noun) /ˈtɒspɒt/ rude
a slightly old-fashioned insult for someone.
'Don't listen to that guy, he's a massive tosspot.'

touch wood (phrase)
if you say touch wood, you hope to have good luck about something you have just said.
'Touch wood we get sunny weather for our BBQ on Sunday.'

'Tom, Dick and Harry'

tower block (noun) /ˈtaʊə blɒk/
a very tall building used for flats or offices.
'They are building a huge tower block right next to my office.'

townie (noun) /ˈtaʊni/ rude
a slightly derogatory term for a young uneducated person who lives in a town or small city (similar to 'chav').
'The pub down the road is always full of townies, whereas this one seems to only attract families.'

trump (verb) /trʌmp/
to pass wind or fart.
A – 'Did you just trump?'
B – 'No, it was the dog!'

trustafarian (noun) /trʌstəˈfeəriən/
a young person from a wealthy background whose trust fund allows them to live an alternative lifestyle without working. They generally choose to live in poorer places than they need to in order to seem cool.
'Let's be honest, Kate and Oscar are total trustafarians. They choose to live in a dodgy part of the city and yet they both went to public school.'

(the) Tube (noun) /tʃu:b/
the Tube is an alternative term for the London Underground.
'The quickest way to get to Hammersmith from here is to take the Tube from Green Park.'

tummy button (noun) /ˈtʌmi bʌtən/
an informal term for navel (also 'belly button').
'It's amazing how much fluff I find in my tummy button.'

TV licence (noun) /ti: ˈvi: laɪsəns/
a licence allowing people to watch and record live TV and BBC iPlayer legally in the UK.
'If you want to watch the BBC, you have to buy a TV licence.'

twat (noun) /twæt/ rude
a vulgar word for a woman's genitals. It's also used as an offensive word for 'idiot'.
'We met Obafemi's new housemate last night and he came across as a bit of a twat if I'm honest.'

twee (adjective) /twi:/
a disapproving way to describe something overly cute, pretty or sentimental.
'I enjoyed our holiday but I found the village we stayed in to be a bit twee.'

twit (noun) /twɪt/ slang
a derogatory term for someone meaning they are silly or stupid.
'Don't be such a twit, Boris, you know your plans will never work.'

two fingers (noun) /tu: ˈfɪŋgəz/
a rude way to show your anger at someone by physically or metaphorically raising your two fingers in a V sign.
'She basically put two fingers up at her boss.'

two-up two-down (noun) /ˈtu: ʌp ˈtu: daʊn/
a small house with two rooms downstairs and two rooms upstairs.
'My grandad was raised in a two-up two-down in Tottenham.'

tyke (noun) /taɪk/
a person from Yorkshire, a county in the north of England.
'I'm a proud tyke, born and bred in Yorkshire.'

U

UCAS (noun) /ˈjuːkæs/
an abbreviation for 'Universities and Colleges Admissions Service'. UCAS organises the admissions process for British universities.
'Have you filled out your UCAS form yet?'

undercarriage (noun) /ˈʌndəkærɪdʒ/ slang
a euphemism for a person's genitals.
'This bike saddle is really uncomfortable on my undercarriage.'

undercrackers (noun) /ˈʌndəkrakəz/ slang
men's underwear.
'Pull up your trousers, dude! I can see your undercrackers.'

(the) Underground (noun) /ˈʌndəgraʊnd/
the most common name for London's underground railway network.
'The best way to get around London is on the Underground.'

under the cosh (phrase)
under pressure or in a difficult position.
'Birmingham City were under the cosh for the entire second half against Manchester United.'

undies (noun) /ˈʌndiz/
short for 'underwear'.
'Khaled, you left your undies in the bathroom. Can you go and pick them up?'

uni (noun) /ˈjuːni/
a short form of 'university'.
'I'm seeing my uni mates this weekend.'

Union Jack (noun) /juːniən ˈdʒæk/
the name of the red, white and blue flag that represents the United Kingdom.
'The Union Jack is flown above the Houses of Parliament.'

unit (noun) /ˈjuːnɪt/
someone who is physically large and impressive.
'Some of these rugby boys are absolute units. Look at the size of their thighs!'

'undercrackers'

TOM'S TIPS

One big distinction between accents in the north and south of England is the /ʌ/ and /ʊ/ sounds. In the South, they say both /ʌ/ and /ʊ/ but in the North, they only use /ʊ/. A phrase like 'up the duff' showcases this perfectly. In the North, it's /ʊp ðə dʊf/ whereas in the South, it's /ʌp ðə dʌf/.

up for (something) (phrase)
an informal way to say you are enthusiastic to do something.
'Are you up for going to Glastonbury next year?'

up sticks (phrase)
to go and live somewhere else.
'At the end of the year, I think we're going to up sticks and move to Australia.'

up (your) street (idiom)
used to talk about something you like doing or are interested in.
'You should go and see Hamilton, it's right up your street.'

up the (something) (phrase)
a phrase used to show support for a group or sports team, e.g. 'up the blues' or 'up the reds'.
'West Ham fans shout 'Up the Hammers!' to show support for their football team.'

'up the duff'

up the duff (phrase) slang
pregnant.
'I didn't know Gigi is up the duff!'

use-by date (noun) /ˈjuːz baɪ deɪt/
the date printed on food containers that indicates the last day the food should be consumed (also 'expiry date').
'When's the use-by date on that box of eggs?'

use your loaf/noggin'/brain (phrase) slang
to use your common sense.
'Mate, don't ask me how to do the task, use your loaf!'

V

VAT (noun) /viː eɪ ˈtiː/
value-added tax. This is the tax paid during the production of goods and services and by the end customer.
'The prices listed on the menu already include VAT.'

veg (noun) /vedʒ/
a short form of 'vegetables'.
'My grandparents have meat and two veg pretty much every night.'

'there's a great veggie restaurant'

veggie (noun) /ˈvedʒi/
an informal term for a vegetarian.
'My mum was a veggie her whole life.'

veggie (adjective) /ˈvedʒi/
an informal term for vegetarian, usually relating to people who don't eat meat or fish, or food that doesn't contain meat or fish.
'There's a great veggie restaurant just round the corner, if you fancy going sometime?'

Victoria Cross (noun) /vɪktɔːriə ˈkrɒs/
the highest honour for bravery in the United Kingdom.
'The Victoria Cross was first presented by Queen Victoria in 1856.'

W

waffle (noun) /ˈwɒfəl/
speech or writing that contains a lot of words without really saying anything interesting or important.
'Goodness, I've never heard so much waffle from one politician.'

waffle (on) (verb) /ˈwɒfəl/
to say or write a lot of words without really saying anything interesting or important.
'Professor Garcia's lectures are really dull. He just waffles on for hours.'

WAG (acronym) /wæg/
stands for 'wives and girlfriends'. A slightly derogatory term that refers to women who are married to or date sportspeople, mainly footballers.
'The England team and their WAGs stayed in a hotel near my town in northern France.'

wag (verb) /wæg/ slang
to miss school deliberately.
'Let's wag school tomorrow and hang out at your house all day.'

wally (noun) /ˈwɒli/
an alternative to 'idiot'.
'You look a right wally in that shirt!'

wanker (noun) /ˈwæŋkə/ rude
a very rude insult for someone you think is stupid or contemptible. It comes from the word 'wank', meaning 'masturbate'.
'Harry, stop behaving like a wanker.'

wanky (adjective) /ˈwæŋki/ rude
stupid or pretentious.
'Holly wants to go to some wanky club for her thirtieth.'

washing-up liquid (noun) /wɒʃɪŋ ˈʌp lɪkwɪd/
the liquid used to clean cutlery and plates in a sink.
'Have we got any more washing-up liquid? I want to do the dishes.'

watering hole (noun) /ˈwɔːtərɪŋ həʊl/
a humorous term for a pub.
'Shall we try and find a good watering hole around here and get out of the rain?'

waz (noun) /wæz/ slang
a slang word for the act of urinating (also 'wazz').
'Where's the loo? I need a waz.'

wazzock (noun) /ˈwæzək/
an informal word for a stupid person.
'Stop acting like such a wazzock, Santiago, and say sorry to Natalia.'

'waffle'

WC (noun) /dʌbəlju: ˈsi:/
an abbreviation of 'water closet', meaning 'toilet'.
'The WC is on the second floor.'

wedding tackle (noun) /ˈwedɪŋ tækəl/ rude
a euphemism for male genitals.
'I accidentally saw his wedding tackle when he got out of the shower.'

wee (adjective) /wi:/
a mostly Scottish term for 'little' or 'small'.
'Can I have a wee bit more tea, please?'

weedy (adjective) /ˈwi:di/
physically weak.
'I was such a weedy little kid at school.'

weegie (noun) /ˈwi:dʒi/ slang
someone from Glasgow (mainly used by people from Edinburgh).
'I lived with a bunch of weegies when I was at med school.'

well (adverb) /wel/
used before adjectives to add emphasis, similar to 'very' or 'really'.
'The new Bond film is well good.'

wellington boots (noun) /welɪŋtən ˈbu:ts/
waterproof rubber boots, usually worn in rainy, muddy conditions (also 'wellies').
'Put on your wellies kids, it's really muddy in the woods.'

wet (adjective) /wet/
having a weak character and lacking strength of personality.
'My dad doesn't like my new boyfriend, he says he's a bit wet and needs to toughen up.'

wet the baby's head (idiom)
to celebrate the birth of a baby by having an alcoholic drink.
'We're going to wet the baby's head on Saturday if you'd like to join us.'

whacked (adjective) /wækt/ slang
very tired.
'I'm really rather whacked. I might go and have a lie-down on my bed.'

whatevs (exclamation) /wɒtˈevz/ slang
used to show a sense of indifference to someone's comment. It's another way to say that you don't care.
A – 'Did you hear Asmita has started dating your ex?'
B – 'Whatevs!'

wheelie bin (noun) /ˈwi:li bɪn/
the large rubbish bin on wheels that is outside a house.
'Charlotte, can you put this rubbish bag straight into the wheelie bin please?'

whiffy (adjective) /ˈwɪfi/
used to describe something that smells bad.
'Wayan, your sports bag is really whiffy. Go and put everything into the washing machine immediately.'

whinge (verb) /wɪndʒ/
to complain about something.
'Kids, stop whingeing! We're nearly home, you can have something to eat when we get there.'

whip-round (noun) /ˈwɪp raʊnd/
when a group of people all put money into a collection in order to buy a gift for someone, e.g. when they leave a job or for their birthday.
'Let's have a whip-round and buy Joyce a goodbye gift.'

‘why aye man!’

Whitehall (noun) /ˈwaɪthɔːl/
a metonym used for the British civil service. It’s a street in London where many of the civil service offices are located.
‘Plans for a new airport near London are being discussed in Whitehall.’

white-van man (noun) /waɪt ˈvæn mæn/
a male driver of a white van, usually driving for work purposes, whose driving is aggressive.
‘I was driving around the ring road and this white-van man cut me up.’

whoopsie daisy (phrase)
a phrase used to acknowledge a mistake, e.g. someone falling over or the spilling of a drink. It was popularised by Hugh Grant in the 1999 film ‘Notting Hill’ (also ‘oops-a-daisy’ and ‘upsie daisy’).
‘Whoopsie daisy! Otis has just spilt his milk on the carpet. Can you get a cloth?’

why aye (man)! (phrase)
an alternative to ‘yes’ or ‘of course’, used largely in the northeast of England.
A – ‘Shall we get a fish supper tonight?’
B – ‘Why aye man!’

wicked (adjective) /ˈwɪkɪd/ slang
an informal word for ‘great’ or ‘brilliant’.
‘I watched a wicked new series on Netflix about hip-hop music.’

wide boy (noun) /ˈwaɪd bɔɪ/ slang
a disapproving term for a young man who is wealthy but who earns it in a dishonest way.
‘James has got a reputation for being a bit of a wide boy.’

windscreen (noun) /ˈwɪndskriːn/
the glass panel at the front of a car.
‘There’s a crack in the windscreen, so I need to get it fixed.’

Windsor Castle (noun) /wɪndzə ˈkɑːsəl/
a famous royal residence in Berkshire, just west of London.
'I really recommend a day trip to Windsor Castle.'

wind (someone) up (phrasal verb) /waɪnd ˈʌp/
to tease or annoy someone.
'Sven, don't wind your brother up and please give him back his hat.'

wind-up (noun) /ˈwaɪnd ʌp/
a false statement said in order to make a joke or tease someone.
'You saw Emma Watson in Sainsbury's? No! That's got to be a wind-up.'

wind-up merchant (noun) /ˈwaɪnd ʌp mɜːtʃənt/ slang
someone who enjoys teasing or annoying other people.
'There's a guy at work who is a complete wind-up merchant. He tries to annoy me on a daily basis.'

wind your neck in (phrase) slang
a slightly rude phrase that can be used to tell someone to mind their own business, stop giving their opinion on something or to shut up.
'You don't know anything about Sarah and Keisha's relationship, so wind your neck in a bit.'

wireless (noun) /ˈwaɪələs/
an old-fashioned word for a radio.
'Turn on the wireless, I think the United game is on.'

wobbly (noun) /ˈwɒbəli/
if you throw a wobbly, you suddenly become very angry or upset.
'Chris throws a wobbly every time I forget to clean the coffee machine.'

wonga (noun) /ˈwɒŋgə/ slang
money.
'Costas has made so much wonga betting on horses over the years.'

Woolyback (noun) /ˈwʊlibæk/
a nickname for people living in the areas just outside Liverpool who then travel into the city (also 'wool').
'Would you describe yourself as a Liverpudlian or a Woolyback?'

worldie (noun) /ˈwɜːldi/
used in a sporting context, a worldie is an excellent performance or amazing goal.
'That Son Heung-Min worldie against Burnley is still my favourite goal of all time.'

wotcha (exclamation) /ˈwɒtʃə/ slang
a very informal greeting similar to 'hey' (also 'wotcher').
'Wotcha Malik, how's life treating you?'

wrinkly (noun) /ˈrɪŋkli/ slang
a humorous term for an old person.
'Look how many wrinklies are queuing up for this music night, don't you think we're a little young to be here?'

write-off (noun) /ˈraɪt ɒf/
a vehicle that has been damaged to the point where it is no longer drivable.
'Our old Toyota is a complete write-off, we'll never get it started again.'

'wrong 'un'

wrong 'un (noun) /ˈrɒŋ ən/ slang
a bad or untrustworthy character.
'Christina only ever seems to date guys you'd class as wrong 'uns.'

Y

yam yam (noun) /ˈjæm jæm/
someone from the Black Country, which is an area of England that includes Wolverhampton, Dudley and Walsall.
'My boss is a yam yam and I love her accent.'

yea big (phrase)
a term used when using your hands to demonstrate the size of an object.
'Her old TV is about yea big. Do you think you have space for it in your flat?'

yellow line (noun) /jeləʊ ˈlaɪn/
a line of yellow paint along the side of a road, indicating that vehicles cannot be parked there at certain times.
'It's only a single yellow line, so we can park here after nine.'

Y-fronts (noun) /ˈwaɪ frʌnts/
underwear worn by males that have a Y-shaped seam at the front.
'All I got for Christmas was a pair of Spider-Man Y-fronts.'

yob (noun) /jɒb/ slang
a young person who behaves in an aggressive, rude way.
'There is always a group of yobs hanging about outside the arcade at night.'

yonks (noun) /jɒŋks/
an informal word meaning a very long time.
'I haven't seen my old headteacher Mrs Jelani for yonks.'

yoof (noun) /juːf/
a non-standard spelling of 'youth'.
'I don't know anything about yoof culture these days.'

Yorkshire pudding (noun) /jɔːkʃə ˈpʊdɪŋ/
a traditional side dish eaten with a Sunday roast. It's a batter consisting of eggs, flour, and milk or water.
'My dad makes the fluffiest Yorkshire puddings in the world.'

young offender (noun) /jʌŋ əˈfendə/
a criminal under the age of 21.
'It's hard for young offenders to re-enter society after they have been released.'

young offender institution (noun) /jʌŋ əˈfendə ɪnstɪˈtʃuːʃən/
a type of prison that is designed to hold young offenders from as young as 15 all the way to 21.
'A lot more funding needs to go into young offender institutions.'

youth hostelling (noun) /ˈjuːθ hɒstəlɪŋ/
the activity of staying in youth hostels and travelling between them.
'We're going youth hostelling around the Lake District in July.'

yummy mummy (noun) /jʌmi ˈmʌmi/
a mother who is very attractive.
'There are quite a few yummy mummies in my book group.'

Z

zebra crossing (noun) /zebrə ˈkrɒsɪŋ/
an area across a road, where pedestrians can cross. Zebra crossings are painted white and black.
'The Beatles walked across a zebra crossing in their iconic "Abbey Road" album cover photo.'

zero-hours contract (noun) /zɪərəʊ aʊəz ˈkɒntrækt/
a fairly modern concept in which the employer isn't obliged to offer the employee a minimum number of working hours per week.
'I'm sick and tired of working in places that only offer zero-hours contracts.'

zimmer frame (noun) /ˈzɪmə freɪm/
the metal frame frail or ill people use to help them have more balance when they are walking.
'They think Grandma is going to need a zimmer frame when she gets out of hospital

'zero-hours contract'

WHAT BRITS SAY AND WHAT THEY ACTUALLY MEAN

As if learning a new language wasn't hard enough, Brits have chosen to add an extra layer of complexity for you. What we say isn't always what we mean. This is an important lesson to learn early because you can avoid years of misunderstandings and confusion. We use certain phrases that may appear to say one thing but in actual fact, the speaker's intention is entirely different. Have a look at this conversation between two Brits.

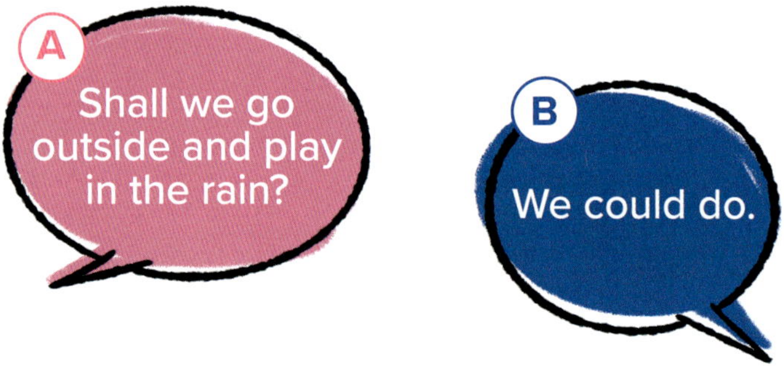

Let's test your ability to decode what this Brit meant. Is B saying...

1) yes, I want to?

2) we literally have the ability to play in the rain?

3) no, I really don't like that idea?

If you chose option 3, you are of course correct. While it might appear that B responded with an affirmative response, 'could do' is actually a subtle way to show a lack of enthusiasm to a suggestion. Now, clearly a lot of meaning lies in the intonation of the speaker, and how they said the phrase must be taken into account. Below are a few light-hearted examples of where a Brit might say one thing but mean another (don't take them too seriously).

alright/you alright? – to the untrained ear, this sounds like the person is asking you about your health and mental wellbeing but really it's just another way to say 'hi'. Answer back with 'alright' and you have navigated another tricky British interaction successfully.

anyone want the last (something)? – imagine one last piece of chocolate cake on the table and someone says 'anyone want the last piece?' It's natural to think they are genuinely offering it to you, but they are not! They want it and they are willing to kill for it. The thing is they don't want to seem rude, so they ask this question. Be careful how you reply. Do you really want that piece of cake? Works equally well with biscuits, chocolates ... anything delicious really.

by the way – if someone introduces a seemingly incidental piece of information by saying 'by the way' it is NOT incidental! It is, in fact, the most important point that they have been wanting to say all along. Here's an example ...

A – 'I'm going to Katie's party on Saturday, are you?'
B – 'Yeah, I'm going.'
A – 'Oh by the way, have you seen my hairdryer anywhere? I left it on the kitchen table.'

What's really going on here? Does A care whether B is going to the party? No! Of course not. All A cares about is where that bloody hairdryer has got to and if B has sneakily borrowed it.

can I have a quick word? – translation: 'you are in trouble'. If someone in your office (or home) asks you if they can have a quick word, start panicking. Nine times out of ten it'll be about something you did wrong, like break the photocopier or make the new flatmate cry. Still, there's always the chance it's that one out of ten job promotion and big bonus news you were dreaming of ... so not all bad.

could do – a perfect way to show a lack of enthusiasm for a suggestion. It's usually followed very quickly by a counter suggestion to move the conversation off the previous idea.

don't let me keep you – one of the all-time great ways to extract yourself from a conversation, either in person or on the phone. At first glance, it seems like a perfectly polite and reasonable thing to say: you are being very considerate of their time. Look closer, and it's actually a brilliant way to say you want this conversation to end. It's YOUR time you are being considerate of, not theirs! You're done with this chat but you present it as if it's them you are thinking of ... this deserves a self-congratulatory pat on the back. Well done, you!

I'd love to, but ... – this is the perfect way to reject someone's invitation politely. It sounds to the invitee like you want to do the activity but you can't, when in actual fact you never had any desire to do it. You can add any excuse after this phrase: 'I'd love to, but I've already got plans'; 'I'd love to, but I have to take my dog for a walk'; or 'I'd love to, but I need to go home and water my plants.' I challenge you to find a more useful phrase in English.

'you must be busy – don't let me keep you!'

I'll bear it in mind – this may sound like the person is going to consider your suggestion but don't be fooled! They've already dismissed it in their mind as a terrible idea and taken you off their Christmas card list.

I'll let you go – a variation of 'don't let me keep you' often used to end a phone call. You'll let me go? How kind of you!

I'll see what I can do – used as a reply to someone's request. Essentially you are saying 'I really can't do what you've asked', either because you genuinely can't or you simply don't want to.

I might see you there – sounds like they are coming, right? Wrong! I'm sorry but they have no desire to come to this party, social gathering, dinner or whatever it is you are talking about. The use of 'might' is what tells us this. If they were coming, they'd say 'I'll see you there' and even then I wouldn't be 100% certain.

I'm not being funny, but ... – get ready for a statement that is definitively not funny (they did warn you) and almost certainly borderline offensive (they didn't warn you). It's frequently employed just before a spicy take like 'I'm not being funny, but DJs aren't proper musicians, they just push buttons.' Uff, spicy!

I'm not entirely sure – when someone responds to your question with 'I'm not entirely sure' it's another way of saying 'I have absolutely no idea'.

interesting – if you hear someone use the word 'interesting' to describe something, half the time they think it's 100% not interesting. Imagine you show a friend your new orange jumper and they say 'Oh, that's interesting!' Uff, I'm sorry to break it to you, but 'interesting' is not what they really think: hideous maybe, interesting definitely not. Brits use it to avoid giving honest negative feedback, because that would be way too direct, right? It's wonderfully versatile and can be used to describe a work presentation, an outfit, a friend's new boyfriend, a late-night text message from an ex ... all could be 'interesting'. Of course, tone and facial expression are key to realising if it's genuine or not.

it's not ideal – Brits are masters of the understatement, and if something is 'not ideal' it's, frankly, a bloody disaster. You ask a friend to dog-sit your furry little pooch and they say 'Erm it's not ideal', they are trying to tell you dog-sitting for you right now might literally ruin their life! Do you want that guilt on your hands? No, I thought not.

make yourself at home – what's this? You think you can behave as if their home is yours? Turn the TV on and put your feet up? Ha! You have been fooled again! Don't under any circumstances think you have free rein to do as you please. You may sit in the designated visitor's chair and you may use the loo (with permission) and that is all. As a visitor you have two jobs: behave and then leave quietly.

sorry – please don't think for one minute that when someone bumps into you on the Tube and then says 'sorry', they are genuinely apologising (OK, they might be sometimes). It's much more likely that they are using 'sorry' to avoid embarrassment and social awkwardness. We Brits use it as a way to smooth out social interactions and avoid conflict. Survival in the UK means deploying a couple of sorries throughout your day, so go forth and unleash a few sorries into the universe – you might quite like it.

that's a brave choice – if you hear this said to you, I'm afraid to say it's not a recognition of your courage. Oh no, it's a sly way of saying 'I would never be so stupid as to make that decision'. Imagine you tell someone you are leaving your high-paying corporate job to become an artist and they say 'oh, that's a brave choice'. They don't think it's brave, they think it's madness!

'that's not bad...'

that's not bad – this may sound negative but in actual fact, it's a positive affirmation that someone likes something. So let's say you make a suggestion in a meeting or show your colleagues a piece of work and they respond with 'that's not bad'; they actually think it's pretty decent. Good job! You can be quietly pleased with yourself.

we should meet up soon – used when you bump into someone you know and you have to make small talk. The only way to exit this situation politely is to promise to 'meet up soon'. Clearly, neither of you have any intention of doing so, ever!

you've caught the sun – translation: 'the sun has burned you to a crisp, you idiot!'

TOM'S TIPS

If someone asks 'How are you?', don't give them your life story: 'Oh I've had a terrible day. I had to take my dog to the vet and then ...' STOP! Just reply with 'Fine, and you?' and move on with your day. The perfect British conversation!

HOW TO PRONOUNCE TRICKY UK PLACE NAMES

I'd like to take this opportunity, on behalf of the British public, to apologise to you.

What for? I hear you ask.

Well, it's for all the times you've had to try to pronounce one of our ridiculous place names and got it wrong. It's not your fault, it's ours! They are like phonetic booby traps, ready to embarrass anyone at any time. Don't worry, we find them tricky too!

One former student of mine speculated that we do it deliberately for our own entertainment. While I agree it would be rather fun, I can promise you we really don't.

So, why are UK place names so tricky to pronounce, even for us locals?

Well firstly, modern English, as we know it, is a wonderful blend of the various languages that have come to these shores with their settlers. The Romans introduced Latin, while the Celts contributed elements of the Celtic languages. In the north, the Vikings left their mark with Old Norse, and then the Angles, Saxons and Jutes came over from northern Europe, creating the bedrock of Old English. Oh, and in 1066 the Normans arrived, bringing French into the mix. What a mighty stew of languages that is. Then you add the magical ingredient of time and this changes everything, because over hundreds of years the relationship between how a word is spelled and how it is pronounced becomes slowly uncoupled.

A great example of this is London's famous River Thames. The word is believed to have come from the Celtic word Tamēsa, meaning dark river. It then evolved into the Latin form Tamēsis, and in parts of Oxfordshire it is still referred to as the River Isis. Over centuries, it morphed again, this time into the shorter form of Tames. In the 1500s, the 'h' was added to the spelling, making it the name we recognise today – the River Thames.

This was done with the mistaken belief that the word 'Thames' originally derived from a Greek river called 'Thyamis'. Despite the spelling change, the pronunciation of the 'th' remained /t/ in line with previous spellings. This has resulted in confused visitors to London often saying it /θeɪmz/ or /θæmez/. Both very reasonable attempts, given the spelling. However, our mighty River Thames is, in fact, pronounced /temz/.

Tamēsa → Tamēsis → Tames → Thames

Confusing? We've only just begun, but don't worry – the good news is there are some helpful patterns we can use to guide us.

Let's start with common suffixes you'll find in place names across the country.

-borough / -burgh / -brough

These three suffixes are common terms for fortified town and are all pronounced either /brə/ or /bərə/, for example Edinburgh is /ˈedɪnbərə/.

EXAMPLES:

Edinburgh

Scarborough

Middlesbrough

Peterborough

Loughborough

-cester

The ending -cester originally meant Roman fort 'castrum' and can be found in many old settlements across the country. This common suffix is articulated as /stə/ with the 'c' being silent, so Leicester is pronounced as /ˈlestə/.

EXAMPLES:

Leicester

Worcester

Gloucester

Towcester

Bicester

-ford

The ending -ford originally indicated a crossing, road or ford. In many British English accents, the /r/ is silent here and we'd use the schwa /ə/ sound on the vowel, so Oxford is /ˈɒksfəd/.

EXAMPLES:

Oxford

Bradford

Stratford

Salford

Chelmsford

-ham

The ending -ham historically referred to a village or homestead and can be found in place names all across the country. When -ham is found as a suffix, it's pronounced by omitting the /h/ and using a schwa /ə/, so Birmingham is pronounced /ˈbɜːmɪŋəm/.

EXAMPLES:

Durham

Nottingham

Cheltenham

Birmingham

Oldham

-mouth

The suffix -mouth indicates the mouth of a river and can be found in a few coastal towns and cities around England. It's pronounced with a schwa /ə/ sound, so Bournemouth is /ˈbɔːnməθ/.

EXAMPLES:

Plymouth

Bournemouth

Exmouth

Portsmouth

Falmouth

-shire

The suffix -shire commonly denotes a modern or historical county in the UK. It's pronounced as /ʃə/ with the schwa /ə/ sound at the end, so Yorkshire is /ˈjɔːkʃə/.

EXAMPLES:

Yorkshire

Lancashire

Derbyshire

Lanarkshire

Worcestershire

-ton

The ending -ton historically referred to a farm or hamlet. It is once again pronounced with that classic British English sound, the schwa /ə/, so Paddington would be /ˈpædɪŋtən/.

EXAMPLES:

Brighton

Kensington

Buxton

Paddington

Wolverhampton

-wich

The suffix -wich commonly denoted a town and can be pronounced without the /w/ sound. The ending can either be /ɪdʒ/ or /ɪtʃ/, so for example Norwich is pronounced /ˈnɒrɪtʃ/ or /ˈnɒrɪdʒ/.

EXAMPLES:

Dulwich

Norwich

Greenwich

Harwich

Woolwich

Llan-

In Wales, a common prefix you'll find on place names is Llan-, which denoted a church or parish. Now the tricky thing here is that the double L in Welsh is pronounced as a voiceless alveolar lateral fricative and does not exist in the English language. So for these examples, you'll have to use your best Welsh.

EXAMPLES:

Llandaff

Llangollen

Llandudno

Llanelli

And if you really want a challenge, have a go at the country's longest place name:

Llanfairpwllgwyngyllgogerychwyrndrobwllllantysiliogogogoch

Yikes! That makes saying Worcestershire look like a piece of cake.

Loch

The final word I'd like to look at is the Scottish word for 'lake' – 'loch'. You'll find this word right across Scotland, most famously Loch Ness, the home of the Loch Ness monster. To say it accurately we must once again employ a sound that isn't commonly used in English and that's the voiceless velar fricative /x/. So Loch Ness would be /lɒx ˈnes/. For some English speakers, the /x/ sound might be replaced by a /k/ to make it easier to say. In Northern Ireland, a fresh water lake is a 'lough' and has the same pronunciation as 'loch'.

EXAMPLES:

Loch Fyne

Loch Ness

Loch Morar

Loch Lomond

Lough Neagh

Hopefully, this section has given you the knowledge you need to go out there and pronounce those tricky UK place names with confidence. Don't forget, we Brits struggle with them too.

TAXI

IT'S A LONDON THING

COCKNEY RHYMING SLANG

Picture this: it's the mid-19th century, and you're wandering the vibrant, bustling streets of London's East End. In amongst the general hubbub, you start to hear a peculiar new form of speech: Cockney rhyming slang. It's a delightful, playful way of talking that involves substituting a word with a phrase that rhymes with it, often with the rhyming part omitted. Its exact origins are somewhat unclear, but it is believed to have been developed by locals as a way to conceal meaning from outsiders and figures of authority, such as the police and landlords. With its playful use of words and its often baffling, cryptic phrases, it quickly became a hallmark of Cockney culture, embodying the wit and street-smarts of this tight-knit community.

So how does it work?

1. Take a phrase like 'apples and pears'.
2. Find a word that rhymes with the last word – 'pears' rhymes with 'stairs'.
3. You have the meaning – 'apples and pears' = stairs.

Let's use it in an example sentence:

I'm just going to pop up the apples (and pears) and get my book.

= 'I'm just going to pop up the stairs and get my book.' (Standard English)

Now it's important to note that we don't always use the full phrase.

It's very common to drop the rhyming word. For example 'Barnet fair' means 'hair' but we only use the word 'barnet'.

= 'I'm going to get my hair cut this afternoon.' (Standard English)

This is by no means a complete list of Cockney rhyming slang. It's simply a sample of the ones I have heard in and around London. The big question is: should you use Cockney rhyming slang? To be honest, probably not. I'd focus your attention on higher-frequency British English vocabulary, but I think it's a really fun and interesting topic to learn about. If you are desperate to use some Cockney rhyming slang in your English, I suggest picking one phrase like 'Rosie Lee' and trying it out just for fun. I personally love being playful with my words and Cockney rhyming slang allows me the creativity to do that. If you want to hear Cockney rhyming slang being used, listen to TV personality and actor Danny Dyer speak, or watch films like 'Green Street' and 'Lock, Stock and Two Smoking Barrels'.

Adam and Eve
believe
'Did you hear Sharon and Phil are getting divorced? I can't Adam and Eve it!'

apples and pears
stairs
'I'm just going down the apples. Do you need anything from the kitchen?'

Aris
arse. This comes from 'Aristotle' which rhymes with 'bottle'. This then connects to 'bottle and glass' which gives us 'glass' rhyming with 'arse'. Phew!
'Get off your aris and help me clean the flat.'

Barnet (fair)
hair
'Mate, what have you done to your barnet? It looks terrible!'

bees (and honey)
money
'I've got no bees until payday.'

bird (lime)
time (in prison)
'My brother did bird for robbing a post office when he was 18.'

bread (and honey)
money
'I'm not making enough bread at the moment to pay the rent.'

Bristol (City)
titty (breast)
'My Bristols don't feel comfortable in this bra.'

brown bread
dead
'When the police found him in his home he was brown bread.

bubble (bath)
laugh
'Are you having a bubble? There's no way you got tickets for Oasis!'

(a) butcher's (hook)
a look
'Shall we have a butcher's at that new Picasso exhibition at the Tate?'

china (plate)
mate/friend
'How are you doing, me ol' china?'

cream-crackered / crackered
knackered (very tired)
'You guys look absolutely cream-crackered. Have you been running?'

currant bun
The Sun newspaper
'Did you know, you can't buy the currant bun in Liverpool?'

Desmond (Tutu)
a 2.2 (a lower second-class UK university degree)
A – 'What grade did you get for your degree?'
B – 'I got a Desmond.'

dicky (bird)
word
'I haven't heard a dicky from anyone today.'

dog and bone
phone
'I'll get on the dog and bone and call the restaurant for you.'

donkey's (ears)
years (a long time)
'I haven't seen my school mates for donkey's.

Hank Marvin
starving
'I'm absolutely Hank Marvin. Is there anything in the fridge?'

Jack Jones
alone or on your own
'Murat has gone out and left me all on my Jack Jones.'

Jimmy (Riddle)
piddle (urination)
'Is there a toilet near here? I'm desperate for a Jimmy.'

(Aunt) Joanna
piano (in a Cockney accent it's pronounced 'pianna')
'I like to play the old Joanna every now and again.'

loaf (of bread)
head
'Use your loaf before you do something stupid like that again.'

'let's have a butcher's'

'don't tell me porkies'

mince (pies) / mincers
eyes
'You took the last donut! I saw it with my own mincers.'

on your tod
alone (originates from a jockey called Tod Sloane)
'I've got to go to the party on my tod because my girlfriend's away.'

Pete Tong
wrong (modern-day Cockney rhyming slang). This is a relatively modern one and is a good example of how new slang phrases develop alongside popular culture. Pete Tong is a well-known British DJ.
'Oh this cake is a disaster, it's all gone Pete Tong.'

pony (and trap)
crap / not very good
'We're absolutely pony at padel but we just love playing it.'

pork pie / porkie
a lie
A – 'Did you eat the last piece of chocolate?'
B – 'No!'
A – 'Don't tell me porkies.'
B – 'Honestly, I didn't!'

rabbit (and pork)
talk
'This geezer has been rabbiting on his phone the entire bus journey at the top of his voice.'

Rosie (Lee)
a cup of tea
'Do you want a cup of Rosie before we start the film?'

Ruby (Murray)
curry
'I'm making a Ruby for dinner if you want some.'

Scooby (Doo)
clue
'I haven't got a Scooby where I left my car keys.'

syrup (of figs)
a wig
'My grandfather used to wear a black syrup.'

treacle (tart)
sweetheart
'Alright treacle, how're your mum and dad?'

whistle (and flute)
suit
'I've gotta buy a whistle for Ezra and Chloe's wedding.'

MODERN LONDON SLANG

Multicultural London English, or MLE as it's also known, is a dialect used by the city's young multi-ethnic citizens. Walk down Oxford Street or take a ride on a local bus and you will be sure to overhear someone speaking MLE. As the name suggests, it is a reflection of the social makeup of the city and its immigrant communities. The words and phrases found in MLE have their roots all over the world, in particular Caribbean patois.

The majority of these words have yet to enter standard dictionaries, in part because of how new they are, so I felt it was important to document them here. They are all slang terms and most commonly found in casual conversational English. A lot of them describe things that relate to the issues of youth culture, like social hierarchy, sex, money and friendship.

In the age of social media, language moves and evolves quickly. This has resulted in many of these terms being adopted by English speakers in other parts of the country across social and ethnic groups. As with Cockney rhyming slang, I would view this section as an insight into the fascinating developments of the language rather than a list of words you must incorporate into your English.

aks (verb)
an alternative way to pronounce 'ask'.
'Let me aks you, why are you still going out with Justine?'

allow (it/that) (phrase)
used to say stop it or leave it (also 'low it').
A – 'I'm going to tell Asha her boyfriend asked me out.'
B – 'No! Allow it! Don't get involved.'

bait (adjective)
obvious.
'Kasim is going to get straight nines for GCSEs, that's so bait!'

bare (adverb)
an intensifier meaning 'very' or 'a lot'.
'There were bare mandem at Brianna's party.'

'bossman'

beef (noun)
a grudge or disagreement.
'There has been beef between these two boxers for years.'

beg (noun)
a person who sucks up to other people in order to be their friend.
'Louis was such a beg. Why did we let him chill with us?'

bennin (verb)
to be doubled-up laughing.
'I went to a comedy event last night and I was bennin the whole time.'

big man ting (noun)
used to assert high status.
'You can't work out with me. The gym is a big man ting!'

blaze (verb)
to smoke marijuana.
'I don't blaze as much as I used to.'

blud (noun)
used instead of 'friend' or 'mate'.
'Yes blud, what's going on?'

bossman (noun)
a respectful term of address for a person, often used with someone you don't know the name of, like a shopkeeper or fast-food vendor.
'I'll have the spicy chicken burger and a grape soda, please bossman.'

braap! (exclamation)
a sound that's made when something good has happened like defeating an opponent in a video game. It's a similar sound to a gun being fired or an engine revving.
'Yes, you beat Sam at Call of Duty. Braap!'

bredrin (noun)
a variation of 'friend'.
'Fabian and Marcus have been bredrins since they were at primary school.'

bro (noun)
a term of address for a male, similar to 'mate'.
'Bro, what time are you coming round for the game?'

buff (adjective)
attractive or hot.
'I've heard Jack's got a buff mate called Leon.'

bun (verb)
to smoke (usually cannabis).
'Come we go bun a joint in the park.'

chirpse (verb)
to chat to someone in a flirtatious manner.
'Has Isaac been trying to chirpse you tonight?'

cotch (verb)
to hang out or relax.
A – 'What are you doing?'
B – 'I'm just cotching at man's yard.'

crease (verb)
to laugh out loud.
'Your karaoke performance had us all creasing, fam!'

creps (noun)
shoes.
'Fam, your creps are fresh! Where did you get them?'

dead (adjective)
not very good, boring.
'My weekends has been dead, fam!'

dry (adjective)
boring.
'This film is dry, let's just play Fortnite instead.'

dun know (phrase)
you already know or you know it.
'Boy, you dun know I'm gonna beat you at FIFA!'

dutty (adjective)
dirty.
'Don't come in man's yard with your dutty trainers on.'

ends/endz (noun)
area or neighbourhood.
'We've got bare fast-food options in my ends.'

fam (noun)
a very close friend.
'Yes fam, let's go Oxford Street.'

fassy (noun)
a derogatory word for someone who lacks courage.
'Come let's tell the headteacher what just happened. Don't be such a fassy!'

feds (noun)
the police.
'There are so many feds by the underground station. Something serious must be going on.'

'yes fam'

TOM'S TIPS

If you want to hear modern London slang and the MLE dialect, check out three British TV shows: 'Top Boy', 'People Just Do Nothing' and 'I May Destroy You'.

finesse (verb)
to steal or take something.
'Bruv, did you finesse those trainers?'

flex (verb)
to show off.
'Did you see AJ flexing his new car around the ends today?'

for real (phrase)
an expression used to show surprise, excitement or shock.
A – Stormzy just announced he's going to release a track with Dave.'
B – 'For real? That's crazy news!'

garms (noun)
clothes.
'I need to get some new garms before my trip to Ibiza next week.'

gassed (adjective)
very excited.
'I'm gassed about our trip to Dubai next month.'

(you) get me? (phrase)
a phrase meaning 'do you understand what I mean or said?'
'Man needs to see some sunshine soon fam, you get me? I'm done with this rain.'

gully (adjective)
cool or excellent.
'Your trainers are gully, fam!'

gyal (noun)
girl.
'There are some peng gyals at my college.'

gyaldem (noun)
a group of girls.
'My gyaldem were looking hot last night.'

heads (noun)
people.
'There were bare heads at the house party last night.'

heavy (adjective)
really good.
'That new Jay-Z tune is heavy.'

hench (adjective)
describes someone who is very muscular.
Mate, you are looking hench! Have you been hitting the gym hard?'

jack (someone/something) (verb)
to rob someone or steal something.
'Did you hear Jay got jacked in Wood Green yesterday?'

jokes (adjective)
funny.
'Your sister is jokes fam.'

leng (adjective)
attractive or good-looking (a synonym of 'peng').
'Nina's new girlfriend is leng.'

link (up) (verb)
to meet up with someone.
'Yo, let's link up next week and get a drink or something.'

'let's link up'

‘oh my days!’

long (adjective)
if something is long, it requires too much effort.
A – ‘Come let’s go Westfield and get McDonald’s.’
B – ‘Westfield? Bro, that’s long! Let’s just go Nando’s on the High Street.’

mad (adjective)
amazing.
‘Yo, that Jude Bellingham goal was mad!’

mad ting (noun)
used as a way to show surprise, amazement or agreement with someone.
‘The men’s 100m final was a mad ting!’

man (pronoun)
used by males as a singular or plural pronoun to replace ‘I’ or ‘you’ (plural).
‘Man doesn’t care if it’s late, Let’s go to the club.’

mandem (noun)
a group of friends.
‘All the mandem are coming to the wedding.’

man like (phrase)
a way to re-affirm or talk about someone.
‘Man like Erling Haaland is scoring mad goals at the moment.’

merk (verb)
to kill someone or defeat someone.
‘I heard Lee merked you at FIFA!’

my guy (phrase)
a close friend or acquaintance.
‘Yes my guy, what you saying?’

my man (pronoun)
used to replace third person singular.
‘My man is getting hench!’

nang (adjective)
impressive or really good.
‘Your freestyle was nang, bro.’

off the hook (phrase)
if something is off the hook, it’s awesome or really cool.
‘That rave in Brixton was off the hook!’

oh my days! (phrase)
used to express shock or surprise.
‘Oh my days! Have you seen that video of those guys walking on the top of skyscrapers without any safety harnesses?’

on my life (phrase)
a phrase used to emphasise that the speaker is telling the truth.
‘On my life, I didn’t take your hairdryer.’

ops (noun)
opponents, often used to refer to a rival gang.
‘I saw bare ops in our endz last night.’

P (noun)
money.
‘I’m earning mad Ps in my new job.’

paigon (noun)
an enemy or friend who lies.
'Don't waste your time with Sam, he's a paigon.'

peak (adjective)
if you have had bad luck or an injustice against you, you could say it's peak.
'We've got a surprise maths test? That's peak, bruv!'

peng (adjective)
hot or good-looking.
'Reggie's older sister is peng, you know!'

piff (adjective)
good or attractive.
'These are some piff chips!'

Rah! (expression)
an expression of surprise.
'Rah! Man City just lost to Crystal Palace!'

ramp (verb)
to mess with or tease someone.
'You met Harry Kane? Don't ramp me, fam.'

rasclart (noun)
an idiot or fool.
'Why did you switch off the light? I'm trying to read my book, you rasclart!'

rinse (verb)
to use something up like battery life or phone data.
'I've totally rinsed my phone battery. Can I borrow your phone to call my mum?'

roadman (noun)
a young male heavily involved in street culture.
'All those boys in my endz want to be a roadman.'

rude boy/rude girl (noun)
a term for a man/woman, which has its origins in Jamaica and ska music culture. These days it is used much more generally as an affectionate term (also 'rudie').
'Yes rude boy, how's it going?'

rush (verb)
to attack someone in a group.
'We got rushed by a bunch of boys in the park and ended up having to run for help.'

safe (exclamation)
used to greet someone, agree, show approval or say goodbye.
'Safe mate, how's things at home?'

screwface (noun)
an angry facial expression.
'Why are you giving me a screwface?'

shook (adjective)
shocked or scared.
'You look shook bruv, what just happened?'

shot (verb)
to sell drugs.
'Reece was shotting when he was a teenager but now he's back in education.'

sick (adjective)
cool, awesome, very good.
'Bro, that is a sick jacket. Where did you find it?'

sket (noun)
a derogatory term for a female who has multiple romantic partners.
'Don't call her a sket, she's not like that at all!'

standard (adjective)
normal.
'The Central line is down again, standard!'

swear down (phrase)
seriously, or 'I'm telling the truth'.
A – 'There's no way you're flying business class!'
B – 'I swear down!'

tonk (adjective)
muscular.
'Janet's new boyfriend is tonk!'

twos (verb)
to share something (also 'get twos on something').
'Can I twos your cigarette?'

wagwan! (exclamation)
a Jamaican patois greeting, like 'What's going on?'.
'Wagwan mandem?'

wallad (noun)
a foolish male.
'That wallad just tried to shoplift and got caught by the police!'.

wasteman (noun)
a derogatory term for a man who doesn't do anything with their life.
'My flatmate is such a wasteman. He needs to get a job, fam!'

yard (noun)
someone's home.
'Come round man's yard and watch the football.'

yute (noun)
a young person.
'The yutes in my area are all wearing North Face jackets now.'

'wagwan!'

BRITISH VS WORLD ENGLISH

BRITISH VS AMERICAN ENGLISH DIFFERENCES

apartment	flat
arugula	rocket
attorney	barrister
baby carriage	pram
bachelorette	hen party
bachelor party	stag party
backpack	rucksack
band-aid	plaster
bangs	fringe
beets	beetroot
beltway	ring road
booger	bogey
broil	grill
cab	taxi

call collect	reverse the charges
candy	sweets
cell phone	mobile phone
check	**bill**
checkers	draughts
checking account	current account
cilantro	**coriander**
cleats	football or rugby boots
closet	**wardrobe**
college	university
cookie	**biscuit**
cotton candy	candy floss
crosswalk	zebra or pedestrian crossing
diaper	**nappy**
downtown	city centre
driver's license	driving licence
drugstore	**chemist's**
drunk driving	drink-driving
eggplant	**aubergine**
elementary school	primary school

elevator	lift
ER	A&E
eraser	rubber
expiration date	expiry date
fall	autumn
fanny pack	bumbag
faucet	tap
federal holiday	bank holiday
field	pitch
fire truck	fire engine
first floor	ground floor
flashlight	torch
freeway or expressway	motorway
freshman	fresher
fries	chips
garbage	rubbish
garbage can	dustbin or rubbish bin
gas	petrol

goaltender	goalkeeper
gotten	got
grade	**mark**
ground meat	minced/mince meat
grunt	squaddie
high school	secondary school
hood	**bonnet**
housing project	council estate
jell-o	**jelly**
jelly (also jam)	jam
knock on wood	touch wood
labour union	**trade union**
ladybug	ladybird
license plate	**number plate**
line	queue
lineup	identity parade
liquid courage	**dutch courage**
liquor store	off-licence
lox	smoked salmon

mail	post
main street	high street
math	maths
mom and pop shop	family business
mononucleosis	glandular fever
movie theatre	cinema
oatmeal	porridge
overalls	dungarees
overpass	flyover
pacifier	dummy
pants	trousers
pantyhose	tights
parentheses	brackets
parking lot	car park
period	full stop
pickup game	kickabout
plastic wrap	cling film

popsicle	ice lolly
potato chips	crisps
powdered sugar	icing sugar
public school	state school
purse	handbag
railroad	railway
realtor / real estate agent	estate agent
recess	break time
restroom or bathroom	toilet or loo
resumé	curriculum vitae (CV)
roommate	flatmate
roster	rota
round trip	return ticket
row house	terraced house
rubber boots	wellington boots
sales clerk	sales assistant
scallion or green onion	spring onion
Scotch Tape	Sellotape

second floor	first floor
semester	term
shopping cart	shopping trolley
sidewalk	pavement
soccer	football
stop light	traffic light
store	shop
stroller	pushchair
subway	underground
suspenders	braces
sweater	jumper
sweat pants	tracksuit bottoms
tempest in a teapot	storm in a teacup
thumbtack	drawing pin
tic-tac-toe	noughts and crosses
tie	draw
traffic circle	roundabout

trash can	bin
truck	lorry
trunk	boot
turn signal	indicator
underwear	pants
uniform	kit
vacation	holiday
vanity	dressing table
vest	waistcoat
windshield	windscreen
wrench	spanner
yard	garden
yard or rummage sale	jumble sale
zee (z)	zed (z)
zip code	postcode
zipper	zip
zucchini	courgette

THE INFLUENCE OF THE WORLD ON BRITISH ENGLISH

English has become a globalised language, not just in its usage by millions of speakers around the world, but also in its composition. It has drawn on influences from every corner of the globe. The result is an ever-evolving language that reflects the interplay of history, culture and migration.

At the heart of it all lies the Old English foundation, the bedrock upon which subsequent layers of linguistic borrowings have been laid. But what are these layers? From the south, we encounter Latin, brought over by the Romans. Their influence linguistically isn't as widespread as one might have imagined, but they did leave lexical treasures like 'verbatim', 'et cetera' (usually abbreviated to etc.) and 'scholar'. This, however, pales in comparison to the influence of French upon the English language. As the Norman Conquest swept Britain in 1066, so did the French language, leaving an unmistakable imprint on English to this day. It is believed that modern English is composed of somewhere between 30 and 40 per cent French words. Gems such as 'cuisine', 'mutton' and 'cul-de-sac' are part of our everyday lexicon.

'cul-de-sac'

The Germanic roots of English go deep and we can find evidence of Old Norse, the language of the Vikings, in words like 'take', 'window' and 'egg'. Furthermore, the wider Germanic family contributed their share to the ever-growing lexicon, with Dutch and other Scandinavian languages leaving their indelible mark on English.

If we turn our attention to contemporary times, we find the influence of empire upon British English. Trading routes to the east brought not only goods, but also new language. That said, there is much of the colonial era that sits very uncomfortably with modern-day Brits. Britain's involvement in the slave trade and the appalling atrocities in India, China and beyond highlight how this language has come at a terrible cost.

One final influence that cannot be understated is the saturation of American pop culture from the 1970s onwards. The TV show 'Friends' changed the way a generation of Brits used stress and intonation to add humour to their words, while hip-hop introduced a plethora of slang words to our vocabulary, like 'off the hook', 'kicks' and 'fly'.

Social media has only made America's impact greater in the last 15 years and it shows no sign of slowing down. Indeed the rise of TikTok, YouTube and Instagram has enabled new words and phrases to disseminate rapidly around the world, in hours rather than years. A new word could be coined in Belfast in the morning and be widely adopted in Melbourne by lunchtime. It's musicians, gamers and YouTubers who are shaping our language these days.

WORDS FROM AROUND THE WORLD

One of the great delights of modern British English is how much of a lexical melting pot it has become. You can find the world in these words, each one helping us describe our lives with more colour and precision.

Take German as an example: in 'doppelgänger', it offers us a way to describe a concept that has no word in English. We could add 'wanderlust', 'zeitgeist' and 'schadenfreude' to that list.

Take Japanese as another example. As Japan's culture and technology permeates around the world, so does its language; from 'karaoke' and 'emoji' to 'umami' and 'futon', we furnish our utterances with words from afar, sometimes without knowing it.

I would guess that most Brits don't know their much-loved condiment, tomato ketchup, has its origins in Chinese, or that the product they use to wash their hair originated in Hindi. Isn't it quite beautiful that these words are embedded in this language as a reminder of how interconnected we all are? Here's a short collection of some of the words modern British English has gained.

al fresco
(Italian)
(adverb/adjective) in the open air.
'It's rare to be able to eat al fresco in the UK, unfortunately.'

breeze
(Spanish)
(noun) a light gentle wind.
'At breakfast there was a beautiful tropical breeze through the hotel.'

buffoon
(Italian)
(noun) a person who behaves in a ridiculous manner.
'Why does Gary always act like a buffoon when we go out?'

cushy
(Urdu/Hindi)
(adjective) used to describe a situation that is very easy and comfortable.
'My sister has got a very cushy job at the BBC.'

déjà vu
(French)
(noun) the strange feeling that you have experienced a situation before.
'When we arrived at the hotel, I had this feeling of déjà vu.'

doppelgänger
(German)
(noun) someone who looks exactly like someone else they are not related to.
'Cherry says I've got a doppelgänger at her work.'

emoji
(Japanese)
(noun) a small digital icon that is used to express emotion.
'Are you the kind of texter that uses emojis?'

ketchup
(Chinese)
(noun) a thick red sauce made of tomatoes.
'I always have ketchup with my chips.'

klutz
(Yiddish)
(noun) a clumsy person.
'I'm such a klutz! I just dropped my tea on the carpet.'

Mecca
(Arabic)
(noun) a central place that people are drawn to.
'Copenhagen has become a mecca for all foodies.'

prima donna
(Italian)
(noun) originally meaning the lead female singer in an opera, it has also become used to describe someone difficult to please who believes they are more important than they actually are.
'Our team is full of prima donnas who seem to care more about themselves than the club.'

marmalade
(Portuguese)
(noun) a type of fruit preserve.
'Ever since I watched the Paddington film, I've been craving a marmalade sandwich.'

mukbang
(Korean)
(noun) a live video on social media in which the host eats while interacting with the audience.
'I've got into the habit of watching mukbangs while having my dinner.'

pyjamas
(Arabic)
(noun) a soft shirt and trousers worn in bed.
'I just bought a very cute pair of pink pyjamas.'

rabona
(Spanish)
(noun) an act in football when the player kicks the ball using one leg wrapped behind their standing leg.
'I can't believe she scored the winning goal with a rabona!'

schmooze

(Yiddish)

(verb) to interact with people in a way that is meant to impress them.

'I spent the night schmoozing with a bunch of TV executives.'

shampoo

(Hindi)

(noun) a liquid soap used to wash hair.

'Can you pick up some shampoo from the supermarket?'

smörgåsbord

(Swedish)

(noun) a variety of different things, usually dishes of food.

'I've prepared a little smörgåsbord of snacks from around the world.'

sommelier

(French)

(noun) a wine expert who helps serve and recommend wines in a restaurant.

'My cousin is training to become a sommelier.'

tariff

(Arabic)

(noun) a tax on imported or exported goods into a country.

'The new tariff rates are unsustainable.'

tsunami

(Japanese)

(noun) a hugely destructive tidal surge caused by an underwater earthquake.

'There are tsunami warning signs all over the island.'

wanderlust

(German)

(noun) the desire to travel and see the world.

'I suffered from an acute sense of wanderlust for all of my twenties.'

BRITISH ACCENTS

BRITISH ACCENTS

Audio for the example sentences in this chapter can be found at **collins.co.uk/eltresources**

There is no one 'British' accent! If I had a penny for every time a student has asked me to help them acquire a 'British' accent, I'd be a rich man – well, I'd be able to afford a cup of tea at the Ritz at the very least. In Britain, we have over 30 different regional accents, each with its own distinctive pronunciation. Towns that are ten miles apart can have widely different pronunciation features. Broadly speaking, in England, accents are divided into two categories: those in the North and those in the South. Meanwhile in Scotland, Wales and Northern Ireland, accents all contain variations between cities or regions. In this section, we explore seven of the most predominant English accents: Received Pronunciation, Cockney, Multicultural London English, Scouse, Mancunian, Geordie and Brummie.

One of the things I love most about accents is how we use them to help construct our identity. An accent can tell you so much about a person. It can indicate where someone is from, their social background, their age, their education, their job, their cultural influences, etc. And yet Britain's relationship with its accents is a complicated one. For example, Received Pronunciation (RP) was once the only accent you would hear on the BBC and was seen as the accent of education and authority. While this mindset has shifted over the years, and regional accents are now heard in all parts of society, this old perception of RP being the 'proper' way to speak still lingers for some. The aim of this section is to give you some background information about each accent, outline the most distinctive features so you can identify them, and then give you some examples of famous people who speak with these accents. It is by no means an exhaustive list, but it can be used as a foundation for anyone who wants to understand the basics. There are example sentences and a list of example words with voice recordings so that you can hear the sounds modelled in each accent and then practise them yourself. Enjoy!

RECEIVED PRONUNCIATION

Received Pronunciation (RP), also called Standard Southern British English (SSBE), is the most commonly studied accent for learners of British English. It has been used for generations by most course books, dictionaries and teachers as the 'standard' model of British English, despite less than 5 per cent of the population of England actually speaking it. There are two main reasons for this: first, it has long been perceived to be the accent of the educated and privileged within British society; and second, it was the accent of the BBC and other media outlets. These two factors have cemented RP's status as the preferred accent for the majority of students learning British English as a foreign language. Unlike other accents, the use of RP is not confined to one geographical area, although it is often associated with the south of England. As such, you can have RP speakers from London, Yorkshire or Scotland. Indeed, as with any accent, RP can vary considerably and has certainly changed a lot over time. We are going to focus on two main forms: traditional 'conservative RP' and the contemporary version known as 'modern RP'. In this section, we will identify the distinguishing features of RP with examples. In the accompanying audio, the example sentences are spoken in a modern RP accent.

1) The trap–bath split – /æ/ and /ɑː/

One feature that clearly distinguishes RP and other southern accents from northern ones is the use of two vowel sounds on 'a', as seen here.

/æ/ – man | hand | can | that | chat | action

/ɑː/ – bath | fast | laugh | chance | glass | ask

It is important to note that because RP speakers can be found across the UK, there may be some local influence on how individuals pronounce certain words.

Track 26

EXAMPLE SENTENCE
'My dance class starts at half-past four.'

2) The T sounds

The T sound in RP is a fascinating one because it has three realisations. We have the true T sound that I'm sure you are familiar with – 'water' /ˈwɔːtə/. We have the glottal T sound – 'water' /ˈwɔːʔə/. And finally, we have the flap T sound – 'water' /ˈwɔːt̬ə/.

Let's start with the glottal T, which can be controversial, with some speakers of RP viewing it as lazy or even uneducated to use in most instances. In conservative RP, a glottal T would never be used; however, it has become more common for speakers of modern RP to incorporate it into their accent. It is most commonly found in the mid-position of a word, e.g. 'Scotland' or 'daughter'.

The third articulation of T is equally as controversial but in a very different way. The flap T is most associated with American English, but through pop culture it has filtered into the modern RP accent. In basic terms, it sounds like the /t/ has been replaced by a soft /d/. Let's hear all three realisations of the T sound:

Track 27

EXAMPLE SENTENCE

'My daughter's flat in Scotland didn't have any hot water.'

3) /i/ vs /ɪ/

At the end of a word with a -y, modern RP uses /i/ whereas conservative RP uses the shortened /ɪ/, e.g. 'very' /ˈverɪ/ or 'happy' /ˈhæpɪ/.

Other words include – city | slowly | really | naughty | Piccadilly | Italy | pretty

Track 28

EXAMPLE SENTENCE

'I walked slowly through the city to Piccadilly.'

4) Yod-coalescence vs yod-retention

In conservative RP, the /j/ sound is present when there is a /uː/ after /t/, /d/ or /s/. However, this has disappeared in modern RP, something we call yod-coalescence. This is when the /j/ sound merges with the preceding consonant to make new sounds like /tʃ/ and /dʒ/.

Conservative RP

tuna	duty	YouTube	opportunity
/ˈtjuːnə/	/ˈdjuːtɪ/	/ˈjuːtjuːb/	/ɒpəˈtjuːnɪtɪ/

Modern RP

tuna	duty	YouTube	opportunity
/ˈtʃuːnə/	/ˈdʒuːti/	/ˈjuːtʃuːb/	/ɒpəˈtʃuːnɪti/

Track 29

EXAMPLE SENTENCE
'There's a super opportunity at YouTube to be a producer.'

5) The tapped R

Received Pronunciation is a non-rhotic accent, which means the /r/ sound is not articulated in two positions: when an R comes before a consonant sound – 'hard' /hɑːd/ – and at the end of words finishing with -r or -re – 'share' /ʃeə/.

In conservative RP, there is something called a tapped R. This is when the tip of the tongue hits the alveolar ridge (roof of the mouth) to pronounce the /r/. This happens when the /r/ is between two vowels, e.g. 'Harry', or after a dental fricative, e.g. 'throw'. In modern RP, the tapped /r/ doesn't exist.

Track 30

EXAMPLE SENTENCE
'The very first time I saw Mary, I knew we were meant to marry.'

6) Smoothing of triphthongs

A triphthong is a collection of vowels that occur together in a word, for example /aʊə/ in 'power'. While /paʊə/ would be the preferred pronunciation of 'power' in modern RP, it is very different in conservative RP. The three sounds become one in a process of smoothing, resulting in 'power' /paʊə/ becoming /pɑː/.

/aʊə/ becomes /ɑː/ – e.g. tower (/taʊə/ = /tɑː/),
power (/paʊə/ = /pɑː/),
shower (/ʃaʊə/ = /ʃɑː/)

/aɪə/ becomes /ɑː/ – e.g. fire (/faɪə/ = /fɑː/),
liar (/laɪə/ = /lɑː/),
inspire (/ɪn'spaɪə/ = /ɪn'spɑː/)

/eɪə/ becomes /ɛː/ – e.g. layer (/leɪə/ = /lɛː/),
player (/pleɪə/ = /plɛː/)

Track 31

EXAMPLE SENTENCE
'I had a shower for an hour.'

7) The foot-strut split – /ʊ/ vs /ʌ/

One of the great distinguishing features of RP and southern accents is the distinction between /ʊ/ vs /ʌ/. This distinction is not made in northern English accents, where the /ʊ/ is always used.

/ʊ/ – put | foot | good | woman | would | could | sugar

/ʌ/ – putt | up | butter | summer | shut | run | Sunday

Track 32

EXAMPLE SENTENCE
'Did you have a good Sunday putting pictures up?'

8) Intonation and speed

Because speakers of RP focus so much of their attention on being clear and understandable, the pace of speech is slow, steady and hardly ever rushed. In terms of intonation, there is a general tendency to rise then fall at the end of a sentence.

This is the case for most RP speakers, although some younger speakers of modern RP might use something called uptalk. This is when the speaker's intonation rises at the end, making their utterance sound like a question. This is believed to be the influence of Australian and American English, although the exact genesis of uptalk is disputed.

SPEAKERS OF MODERN RP

Emma Watson, Claudia Winkleman, Gemma Chan, Tom Holland, Louis Theroux, Simone Ashley and Emma Raducanu.

SPEAKERS OF CONSERVATIVE RP

Sir David Attenborough, Dame Joanna Lumley, Dame Judi Dench, Dame Mary Berry, Prince William and Princess Catherine.

COCKNEY

Cockney is the traditional accent of the working class in London. Strictly speaking, to be considered a true Cockney you have to be born within the sound of the Bow Bells, which are located in St Mary-le-Bow church in the Cheapside area of London. A study was undertaken in 2000 to see how far the bells could be heard and it concluded that if you were born six miles to the east of the church, five miles to the north, three miles to the south, and four miles to the west, you were a Cockney. These days, while the Cockney accent is associated with the East End of London, it has migrated from its original roots as many working-class Londoners left the city for the home counties, e.g. Essex, Hertfordshire and Kent.

Cockney is much more than just an accent, it's an entire culture as we saw earlier with Cockney rhyming slang. The Cockney accent has been captured in numerous films over the years: 'Lock, Stock and Two Smoking Barrels', 'Legend' and rather less successfully by Dick Van Dyke in 'Mary Poppins'. It can also be heard on one of Britain's best-loved soap operas, 'EastEnders', which is set in a fictitious area of east London called Walford. Here we look at the main pronunciation features of the accent and identify what it is to sound like a true Cockney.

1) Glottal T

This is perhaps the quintessential feature of the Cockney accent. Any T in the mid or final position is articulated with a glottal stop. This means the airflow is stopped in the vocal folds and is not released, creating the glottal stop. Phonemically, it is represented by /ʔ/ so 'water' pronounced with a glottal T would be /ˈwɔːʔə/. It's important to note that a glottal T cannot be used on a T at the front-position of a word, e.g. top. The act of glottalisation also occurs with /p/ and /k/, e.g. 'paper' /ˈpeɪʔə/ and 'like' /laɪʔ/.

Mid-position words – water | daughter | hotter | better | later | bottle

End-position words – that | hot | sat | flat | tracksuit | bat

Track 33

EXAMPLE SENTENCE
'The hotter the water, the better it is.'

2) Th-fronting

In Received Pronunciation and other UK accents, there are two sounds for 'th': /θ/ (throw) and /ð/ (this). However, in Cockney, voiceless /θ/ is replaced with a /f/ sound, e.g. 'thing' /fɪŋ/, 'bath' /bɑ:f/ and 'Thursday' /ˈfɜ:zdi/. The voiced /ð/ sound on 'th' is replaced by /v/ so 'other' would be pronounced /ˈʌvə/.

/f/ on 'th' – thing | think | bath | thanks | throw | birthday | tooth | healthy

/v/ on 'th' – other | brother | mother | although | clothes | together | weather

Track 34

EXAMPLE SENTENCE
'I think it was my mother's birthday the other day.'

3) /h/ dropping

It is common for a Cockney speaker to drop Hs at the beginning or middle of a word. For example 'help' /elp/, 'hospital' /ˈɒspɪtəl/ and 'behave' /bɪˈeɪv/.

Track 35

EXAMPLE SENTENCE
'I need some help getting Harry to the hospital.'

4) L-vocalisation

A very distinctive feature of Cockney is something called L-vocalisation. When an /l/ occurs a) after a vowel, b) before a consonant in the same syllable, or c) as a syllable itself, it becomes a vowel sound. This sound can vary depending on the speaker, and to many people, the sound that best represents L-vocalisation is actually a semivowel /w/, which is how I have transcribed it phonetically.

a) 'full' /fʊw/ – 'tall' /tɔ:w/ – 'Paul' /pɔ:w/

b) 'milk' /mɪwk/ – 'help' /hewp/

c) 'bottle' /ˈbɒʔəw/ – 'table' /ˈteɪbəw/

Track 36

EXAMPLE SENTENCE
'I've given Paul the milk bottles to put on the table.'

5) Yod-dropping

There is a tendency to drop the /j/ sound on /uː/ when it comes before /t/ and /d/, e.g. 'Tuesday' /ˈtuːzdi/, 'news' /nuːz/ and 'due' /duː/.

Track 37

EXAMPLE SENTENCE
'I've got to get a new one by Tuesday.'

6) -ing /ɪn/ and -thing /ɪŋk/

It is common in Cockney for words ending -ing to be pronounced /ɪn/, e.g. 'singing' /ˈsɪŋɪn/ and 'running' /ˈrʌnɪn/.

On words that end -thing, it is common for an /ɪŋk/ to occur at the end of the word, e.g. 'something' /ˈsʌmfɪŋk/ and 'anything' /ˈenifɪŋk/.

Track 38

EXAMPLE SENTENCE
'She loves singing anything at karaoke.'

7) /r/ as /w/

For some speakers of Cockney, but certainly not all, there is a tendency to replace the /r/ sound with a labiodental /w/ sound, e.g. 'alright' /ɑːˈwaɪʔ/ or 'really' /ˈwɪəliː/.

Track 39

EXAMPLE SENTENCE
'I don't remember nothing, is that alright?'

8) /aː/

Cockney follows the same pattern as many southern English accents and RP by having a broad /ɑː/ sound on many words like 'bath', 'laugh', 'after', 'banana', etc.

Track 40

EXAMPLE SENTENCE
'I've only eaten half a banana this afternoon.'

9) Diphthongs

There is a tendency for Cockney speakers to have broader vowel sounds than RP speakers. They are generally articulated with a wide mouth position, so a word like 'how' would be /æəw/.

/aʊ/ is pronounced /æə/ or /æʊ/, e.g. 'how' /æəw/, 'now' /næʊ/ or 'allow' /əˈlæʊ/.

/eɪ/ is pronounced /æɪ/, e.g. 'paper' /ˈpæɪʔə/, 'train' /træɪn/ or 'plane' /plæɪn/.

Track 41

EXAMPLE SENTENCE

'How much paper do you need?'

10) Double negatives

Unlike standard English, double negatives are a common feature in Cockney syntax. It is not an error, simply a non-standard variation. They occur when two negatives are used in the same clause to express a single negative idea.

Track 42

EXAMPLE SENTENCES

'I didn't see no one' (meaning 'I didn't see anyone').

'We ain't got nothing' (meaning 'We haven't got anything').

SPEAKERS OF COCKNEY

Danny Dyer, Ray Winstone, Stacey Solomon, Thomas Skinner, Alex Scott, Jessie J and Micky Flanagan.

MULTICULTURAL LONDON ENGLISH

Multicultural London English, or MLE as it's also known, is the youngest of all the UK accents, having only really developed in the last 40 years or so. It is the perfect representation of contemporary London: young, diverse and constantly evolving. It is the accent of the city's young multi-ethnic citizens and has pronunciation features that reflect this. It is also heavily influenced by the traditional working-class Cockney accent. MLE can be heard all across London and indeed it has travelled, via social media, to other major urban areas in Britain, where its influence is felt by young people.

1) The price vowel – /aɪ/

One of the most distinctive sounds in MLE is the /aɪ/ in words such as 'fly', 'like' and 'try'. The articulation for many MLE speakers is with a wider mouth position, and the double vowel sound becomes closer to a monophthong. So 'like' would be /laɪk/ and 'price' is /praɪs/.

Track 43

EXAMPLE SENTENCE
'Yo, that price ain't right.'

2) Goose fronting

This is the movement of the /u:/ sound so that it is articulated at the front of the mouth on words like 'food' /fu:d/ and 'you' /ju:/.

Track 44

EXAMPLE SENTENCE
'What food have you got in the fridge?'

3) Th-fronting

One of the main distinctions between MLE and all other British English accents is the pronunciation of 'th'. While it can follow the th-fronting pattern of Cockney, where the voiceless /θ/ becomes /f/ and the voiced /ð/ turns into /v/, it also has its own unique articulation. The best example of this is when /θ/ transforms into /t/ in 'thing' /tɪŋ/. For other words with /θ/ like 'three', 'thanks' and 'thin' speakers would generally lean towards /f/ over /t/. The other pattern to note is the use of /d/ instead of /ð/ so that 'there' becomes /deə/ and 'this' becomes /dis/.

/t/ on 'th' – thing | think | thanks

/d/ on 'th' – there | this | that | those | brother | mother

Track 45

EXAMPLE SENTENCE
'I didn't say it like that though!'

4) Glottal T

The T is such a distinctive part of British English and it's no different in MLE. Generally speaking, it is articulated with a glottal stop, which means the air is restricted by the vocal folds. Just as in Cockney, you'll find words like 'butter' pronounced /ˈbʌʔə/ or 'water' as /ˈwɔːʔə/. This varies from speaker to speaker and indeed from sentence to sentence as to whether someone will use the true T or the glottal T. It's perfectly plausible to use both in the same sentence.

Track 46

EXAMPLE SENTENCE
'I've got a lot of little things to do today.'

5) /h/ dropping

Unlike Cockney, the /h/ sound is often pronounced for example 'happy' is /ˈhæpi/ and 'horse' is /hɔːs/. There are instances in which it might be dropped, such as 'have' /æv/. However, this can often depend on the individual speaker, who may or may not decide to drop the /h/.

Track 47

EXAMPLE SENTENCE
'We booked a really nice hotel for our holiday.'

6) /ɑː/ and /æ/

Because MLE is a southern English accent, it follows the same pattern as RP and Cockney, so there is a distinct difference between /ɑː/ and /æ/.

/ɑː/ – laugh | half | class

/æ/ – hand | fam | gas

Track 48

EXAMPLE SENTENCE
'Half those girls are in my class fam.'

7) /aʊ/

Another diphthong that transitions closer to a single vowel is the /aʊ/ sound. It's found on words like 'how' and 'about', which would be articulated as /haʊ/ and /əˈbaʊt/.

Track 49

EXAMPLE SENTENCE
'Swear down, there's a mouse somewhere in this house.'

8) Stress patterns

Stress plays a very noticeable role in the spoken English of MLE. Speakers will often use heavy stress on certain syllables to emphasise what they are saying or make something clearer. For example adjectives of opinion will often be heavily stressed, e.g. 'That's PEAK, blood!'

SPEAKERS OF MULTICULTURAL LONDON ENGLISH
Stormzy, Little Sims, AJ Tracey, Emile Smith-Rowe, Akala and Mo Gilligan.

SCOUSE

Liverpool, as a city, has a very proud and unique identity. Famously home to the Beatles and two huge football clubs, Everton and Liverpool, it also has one of the most distinctive accents in the UK. Known as 'Scouse', the accent is heavily influenced by the Irish migrants who came to Liverpool in the nineteenth and twentieth centuries. It has pronunciation features found in other northern accents as well as a few sounds not found elsewhere.

1) /x/ as /k/

One of the most distinctive sounds of a Scouse accent is the /x/ sound. It is used to replace the /k/ sound when it appears at the end of a word or syllable, e.g. 'back' /bæx/, 'clock' /klɒx/ and 'tracksuit' /ˈtræxsuːt/.

Track 50

EXAMPLE SENTENCE

'I'll have chicken and chips and a can of coke, please.'

2) /ð/ as /d/

Another quite unique feature of Scouse, which is an influence from Irish English, is on words with the voiced /ð/ sound. They can be realised with a /d/ so for example 'there' /ðeə/ becomes /deə/ or 'that' /ðæt/ becomes /dæt/.

Track 51

EXAMPLE SENTENCE

'She didn't put that there, did she?'

3) /t/ as an affricate

The /t/ sound can be pronounced with an aspirated /s/ sound so that a word like 'start' would sound like /stɑːts/ and 'tea' would be /tsiː/.

Track 52

EXAMPLE SENTENCE

'I'm popping into town to buy some tea.'

4) /h/ dropping

It's common for many Scouse speakers to drop the /h/ sound just like in Cockney, so 'hotel' would become /əʊˈtel/.

Track 53

EXAMPLE SENTENCE
'I've booked a hotel by the harbour.'

5) Final /t/ as /h/

Whereas in most British accents the /t/ sound is often glottalised, in Scouse it can be replaced with /h/. So 'it' would sound like /ɪh/ or 'that' would sound like /dæh/.

Track 54

EXAMPLE SENTENCE
'Wait one minute and I'll show you that hat I was talking about.'

6) Tapped /r/

Scouse speakers have a tendency to make a tapped /r/. That means that the tip of the tongue touches the roof of the mouth quickly. This would be found in words like 'right', 'road', 'very', etc.

Track 55

EXAMPLE SENTENCE
'Take the road on your right and go round the roundabout.'

7) Intervocalic /t/

When a /t/ is found between vowels it can be pronounced as a flapped /r/. There was a celebrity from Liverpool called Cilla Black and her catchphrase was 'a lorra lorra laughs'. The 'lorra' part was her Scouse pronunciation of 'lot of' in which the /t/ became a flapped /r/.

Track 56

EXAMPLE SENTENCE
'What a lot of fun we've had.'

8) /ɜː/

The /ɜː/ sound is pronounced quite distinctly in Scouse. The sound is made further forward in the mouth, with the tongue positioned at the front instead of drawing back as it does in RP. This affects words like 'sir', 'fur', 'bird', etc.

Track 57

EXAMPLE SENTENCE
'That's the third bird I've seen in my garden today.'

9) Two different /əʊ/ realisations

Unlike in RP where the tongue sits in the middle of the mouth for the /əʊ/ sound, Scouse has two alternative realisations. One where the tongue is at the back and one where the tongue is at the front of the mouth. So words like 'no', 'go' and 'throw' can be pronounced in two different ways depending on the speaker.

Track 58

EXAMPLE SENTENCE
'I didn't know there was snow in Spain.'

10) Other vowel sounds

As with other northern English accents, there is no vowel difference between 'trap' and 'bath' so /æ/ is used for both. Equally the /ʌ/ sound is not used, so words like 'sun', 'run' and 'shut' all have a /ʊ/ sound.

Track 59

EXAMPLE SENTENCE
'We had a right laugh on Sunday at Mum's birthday.'

SPEAKERS OF SCOUSE
Jodie Comer, Trent Alexander-Arnold, Abbey Clancy, John Bishop, Steven Gerrard, Jamie Carragher, Mel C, Wayne Rooney and Katarina Johnson-Thompson.

MANCUNIAN

The Mancunian (or Manc) accent is spoken in Manchester, a city in the northwest of England. It is perhaps one of the country's best-known accents, largely because of the exposure given to it by popular ITV soap 'Coronation Street' and famous Mancunians like Noel and Liam Gallagher from Oasis. It has a distinct nasal quality to it and follows similar pronunciation patterns as other northern English accents. That said, it is quite different from the Scouse accent of Liverpool despite the cities only being 30 miles apart.

1) /ʌ/ and /ʊ/

One of the biggest differences between accents in the north and south of England is the /ʌ/ and /ʊ/ sounds. Mancunian speakers would use /ʊ/ for words like 'up', 'tough' and 'but'.

Track 60

EXAMPLE SENTENCE
'Alright love, can you help me get this cupboard up the stairs?'

2) /æ/ and /ɑː/

As with other northern English accents, the Mancunian accent doesn't follow the 'trap–bath' split so it uses /æ/ for words like 'laugh', 'bath', 'grass' and 'dance'.

Track 61

EXAMPLE SENTENCE
'I love a dance and a laugh with my mates on a Friday night.'

3) /h/ dropping

In line with many other accents in the UK, the /h/ tends to be dropped at the beginning of words or in the middle position, e.g. 'behind', 'hotel' and 'hang out'.

Track 62

EXAMPLE SENTENCE
'Manchester United are behind at half time.'

4) /e/ on final 'y'

In RP words like 'lazy' or 'easy' end with an /i/ sound, whereas in Mancunian the final vowel is pronounced as more of an /e/.

Track 63

EXAMPLE SENTENCE
'That was a really easy game for City.'

5) Th-fronting

Like some other UK accents, there is a degree of th-fronting in Mancunian, so that the voiceless /θ/ can become /f/ and the voiced /ð/ turns into /v/.

/f/ on 'th' – thing | thanks | healthy

/v/ on 'th' – brother | weather | either

Track 64

EXAMPLE SENTENCE
'I think the weather is going to get better this weekend.'

6) -ing as /ŋg/ or /n/

There are two main articulations of the -ing. It can either be /ŋg/ – for example 'sing' /sɪŋg/ – or it can be /n/ – for example 'singing' /ˈsɪŋɪn/.

Track 65

EXAMPLE SENTENCE
'Are you thinking of singing at the school talent show?'

7) Glottal /t/

The /t/ sound is often glottalised in a Mancunian accent. As with other accents, it can be found occurring in the middle and final positions, so 'butter' is pronounced /ˈbʊʔə/ and water is /ˈwɔːʔɒ/.

Track 66

EXAMPLE SENTENCE

'Can you pass me a bottle of water?'

8) Other vowel sounds

One of the more distinctive sounds in Mancunian is how the final unstressed syllable is articulated. In RP and other accents, words like 'better', 'later' and 'brother' have a schwa /ə/ sound on the final syllable whereas in Mancunian it can sound more like an /ɒ/.

Track 67

EXAMPLE SENTENCE

'I saw your mother and brother at the sports centre.'

SPEAKERS OF MANCUNIAN

Liam and Noel Gallagher, Aimee Lou Wood, Marcus Rashford, Nick Grimshaw, Jason Manford, Brian Cox, Ella Toon, Gary Neville, Michelle Keegan, Shaun Ryder and John Cooper Clarke.

GEORDIE

The Geordie accent, found in and around the vibrant city of Newcastle upon Tyne in the northeast of England, is one of the most distinct in the UK. It has a unique melody and consonants can sometimes go on a little holiday as speakers sing the stories of the northeast. The people are known for being warm, friendly and having a good sense of humour, so it's no wonder they also have a wonderful accent to match. The term Tyneside English is used to describe the dialect found in the surrounding conurbation, which includes Gateshead and North and South Shields. Let's look at a few of the more discernible pronunciation features.

1) The schwa /ə/ often replaced by /æ/

On words ending in -er and -or, it's common for most British English accents to use a schwa /ə/ sound. However, in Geordie, a near-open central vowel is used that sounds very similar to an /æ/. You'll hear it on words like 'water', 'better' and 'doctor'.

Track 68

EXAMPLE SENTENCE
'My sister is a better singer than you!'

2) The /h/ sound

Unlike most other British English accents, the /h/ sound is often pronounced in a Geordie accent. This is best exemplified in the classic Geordie phrase 'Howay!' which means 'Come on' or 'hurry up!' The /h/ sound is present and fully pronounced.

Track 69

EXAMPLE SENTENCE
'Howay! We're going to be late for our hospital appointment.'

3) The glottalisation of /t/, /p/ and /k/

One of my personal favourite features of a Geordie accent is the frequent glottalisation of three sounds: /t/, /p/ and /k/. We've seen the glottal /t/ many times in other accents, so I'd like to focus more on the presence of the glottal stop on /p/ and /k/. When we find these sounds in the middle of words, they are often dropped, so 'baker' is /ˈbeɪʔæ/. Other words that might have the /k/ dropped are 'working', 'poker' and 'monkey'. The same goes for words with /p/, such as 'happy' /ˈhæʔi/ and 'happen' /ˈhæʔən/.

Track 70

EXAMPLE SENTENCE
'My daughter is so happy working as a baker for Greggs.'

4) /aʊ/ as /uː/

This is perhaps the most well-known feature of a Geordie accent. The diphthong /aʊ/ in words like 'mouth', 'town' and 'down' is realised as /uː/. 'Town' in particular is a word associated with Newcastle and its unique pronunciation /tuːn/.

Track 71

EXAMPLE SENTENCE
'I'm gannin' down the town.'

SPEAKERS OF GEORDIE
Ant and Dec, Jade Thirlwall, Alan Shearer, Cheryl, and Sarah Millican.

BRUMMIE

As a city, Birmingham is wedged between the industrial cities to the north and the home counties to the south and its geography plays a huge part in shaping the people and the accent. I think it's fair to say that Brummie has its fair share of detractors from other parts of the UK, but I have found on my travels that this has only made the local people even more proud of their city and accent. As we look at specific pronunciation features, we'll see influences from both the north and the south, as well as some wonderfully unique features that belong just to Brum. One thing you'll notice when listening to the accent is that it has relatively flat intonation. It can sound quite monotone at times, with drawn out long vowel sounds.

1) /eɪ/ as /aɪ/

One of those sounds that clearly stands out in the Brummie accent is the vowel change on words with /eɪ/, e.g. 'take', 'make', 'favourite'. In a Brummie accent, these words would be made with something closer to an /aɪ/ sound. So 'take' would be /taɪk/ and 'bake' would be /baɪk/.

Track 72

EXAMPLE SENTENCE
'How long did it take to bake that cake?'

2) /aɪ/ as /ɔɪ/

Another diphthong switch that is uniquely Brummie is the use of /ɔɪ/ on words that you might expect to find an /aɪ/. So if we take the word 'like' it might be articulated as /lɔɪk/ or 'alright' could be /ɔ:lˈrɔɪt/.

Track 73

EXAMPLE SENTENCE
'I really like your new bike.'

3) The schwa /ə/ often replaced by /æ/

It's possible for some Brummie speakers to articulate the schwa /ə/ sound at the end of a word as an /æ/. In many British English accents, a schwa is used on words that end with an -er, -or and -a; however, in Brummie it could be pronounced with an /æ/, for example 'player' /ˈpleɪæ/ or 'better' /ˈbetæ/.

Track 74

EXAMPLE SENTENCE
'I'm a better player than my sister.'

4) Glottal T

Not uniquely a Brummie sound, the glottal T can be heard on Ts in the middle and end positions of a word, e.g. matter /ˈmæʔə/.

Track 75

EXAMPLE SENTENCE
'Are you coming to the party on Saturday?'

5) /ʊ/ and /æ/

Two features that link the Brummie accent to the north is the use of /ʊ/ on words like 'cup', 'enough' and 'up', and /æ/ on 'ask', 'laugh' and 'bath'. These are sounds we've seen in Scouse, Mancunian and Geordie as well.

Track 76

EXAMPLE SENTENCE
'I grew up in Brum and then moved to London after uni.'

6) The /g/ in -ng words

A feature that is quite unique to Birmingham is the articulation of /g/ when there is an -ng in a word, e.g. 'sing' /sɪŋg/ and 'hang' /hæŋg/.

Track 77

EXAMPLE SENTENCE
'I learned to sing at the Royal Birmingham Conservatoire.'

7) /iː/ as /eɪ/

Our last feature that we'll look at is the use of the diphthong /eɪ/ on words that have the /iː/ sound. This can happen in the mid-position or on -y endings. For example, 'see' /seɪ/, 'free' /freɪ/ and 'receive' /rɪˈseɪv/.

Track 78

EXAMPLE SENTENCE
'I really hope we see you at the meeting tonight.'

SPEAKERS OF BRUMMIE
Jack Grealish, Alison Hammond, Jude Bellingham, Cat Deeley, Julie Walters, Mike Skinner (The Streets), Tommy and Arthur Shelby ('Peaky Blinders').

'On my YouTube channel, Eat Sleep Dream English, I've analysed the accents of a wide range of famous British people, including: Harry Styles, Adele, Emma Watson, Stormzy, David Beckham, Jodie Comer, Danny Dyer, Tom Holland, Alex Turner, Gemma Chan, Liam Gallagher, Hagrid from Harry Potter and the Peaky Blinders.'

Teacher Tom

OTHER ACCENTS IN THE UK

As I mentioned earlier, you'll find a huge variety of accents up and down the United Kingdom. We've looked at seven in some depth, so now I'd like to touch on a few others to give you a broader understanding.

For learners of English, and curious anglophiles, I think it's really valuable to learn about the pronunciation features of different accents. I also think it's really fun and opens a window into local cultures. As soon as you travel around the UK, you realise just how much variation there is. So, if you are familiar with the possible sounds you might hear, you'll have a greater chance of understanding the people you meet.

Scottish English accents

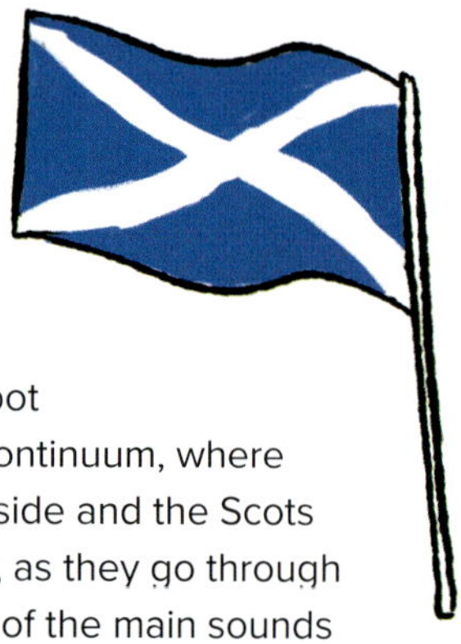

From the urban centres of Glasgow and Edinburgh to the Highlands and remote islands, Scotland boasts a wealth of accents and dialects all with their own unique charms. To attempt to summarise them all here would be simply foolish, so instead I'd like to provide a brief overview of the main distinguishing features. You see, Scotland is home to three official languages – English, Scots and Scottish Gaelic – making it a melting pot of influences. Some linguists talk about a Scottish English continuum, where speakers move between Standard Scottish English on one side and the Scots language on the other, fluidly and somewhat unconsciously, as they go through their day (thescottishsoundschool.com). Let's explore a few of the main sounds you might hear in Scottish English and you can listen to the examples below.

1) The rhotic R

One feature that you might encounter north of the border is the /r/ sound which features much more prominently than in accents south of the border. That's because the R is rhotic in Scotland, which means it is pronounced in a post-vocalic position; for example, 'car' is /kɑ:r/ and 'bird' is /bɜ:rd/.

Track 79

EXAMPLE SENTENCE
'I find it really hard to write birthday cards.'

2) The tapped R

For some speakers, there is a tendency to use a tapped /r/ sound which involves the tongue tapping the alveolar ridge as it makes the /r/ sound.

Track 80

EXAMPLE SENTENCE

'Have you ever tried climbing one of the munros around here?'

3) /ɪ/ as /e/

There are fewer vowel sounds in Scottish English than in the English found south of the border. In total there are nine monophthongs and three diphthongs, many of which are employed differently. One such example is the /e/ sound, which is commonly found on words with an 'i'. So for example, 'bit' is articulated closer to /bet/ and 'in' might be /en/, although this is not true for all Scottish speakers.

Track 81

EXAMPLE SENTENCE

'I've just received a great bit of news from my sister.'

4) /ɒ/ as /ɔ/

Another shift in vowel sounds is the use of /ɔ/ on words that take /ɒ/ in other British English accents. For example 'off' becomes /ɔf/ and 'robot' would be /ˈrəʊbɔt/.

Track 82

EXAMPLE SENTENCE

'I've got a lot going on right now.'

5) The /ʍ/ sound

This is one of those sounds that grounds you squarely in Scotland and yet it isn't used as widely as you might expect. It's the voiceless labial-velar fricative /ʍ/ that some speakers might use on words with Wh- so for example 'which' /ʍɪtʃ/ and 'why' /ʍaɪ/.

Track 83

EXAMPLE SENTENCE

'Do you know where you are going?'

Welsh English accents

In Wales, we find accents that are distinguishable by their melodic intonation. Welsh English is influenced by the Welsh language and there is a wonderful sing-song nature to the intonation of Welsh English that is unlike any other British accent. Let's delve into some of the pronunciation features you might encounter here.

1) Gemination of consonants

One of the most distinctive features of a Welsh English accent is the gemination of consonants. This essentially means a consonant is doubled when it comes after a stress vowel so 'city' would be /ˈsɪt:i/ and 'honey' would be /ˈhʌn:i/.

Track 84

EXAMPLE SENTENCE
'What's your favourite city?'

2) Yod-dropping

It's common for speakers with a Welsh accent to drop the /j/ sound when it appears when an /u:/ comes before /t/ and /d/, e.g. 'Tuesday' /ˈtu:zdeɪ/, 'news' /nu:z/ and 'due' /du:/.

Track 85

EXAMPLE SENTENCE
'The news of my promotion is due on Tuesday.'

3) The tapped R

As with Scottish English, the tapped /r/ is used in Welsh English accents on words like 'right', 'rabbit' and 'around'.

Track 86

EXAMPLE SENTENCE
'Are you alright to come round later?'

Northern Irish English accents

Moving across the Irish sea to Northern Ireland, we find accents heavily influenced by Scottish settlers in the 17th century and of course Irish English. Let's look at a few pronunciation features these Northern Irish accents have in common.

1) /aʊ/ as /aɪ/

The most well-known pronunciation feature of Northern Irish accents is the articulation of the /aʊ/ diphthong. It sounds similar to an /aɪ/ so 'how' might be /haɪ/ and 'house' might be /haɪs/. Other Northern Irish accents might use /ɔɪ/ in both examples.

Track 87

EXAMPLE SENTENCE
'How are you feeling now?'

2) Rising intonation

There is a tendency to use rising intonation much more frequently across an utterance than in most UK accents. Speakers commonly go up at the end of a sentence or clause, making Northern Irish quite identifiable.

Track 88

EXAMPLE SENTENCE
'I think we'll win the game one nil.'

3) /ɪŋ/ as /ɪn/

As with a number of accents in the UK, the 'g' at the end of -ing is often dropped so the sound becomes /ɪn/. For example, 'singing' becomes /ˈsɪŋɪn/ and 'running' becomes /ˈrʌnɪn/.

Track 89

EXAMPLE SENTENCE
'We're going hiking if you want to come.'

PRACTICE

Exercise 1

INITIALS

What do the initials stand for?

1. People can write to their local MP about problems where they live.

A. MEMBER OF PARLIAMENT | B. MAIN PARTNER | C. MAJOR POLITICIAN

2. He had his operation done on the NHS, not privately.

A. NURSES AND HOSPITALS SOCIETY | B. NEED HELP? SHOUT! | C. NATIONAL HEALTH SERVICE

3. Phone for sale, £100 ono.

A. ONE NICE OWNER | B. OR NEAREST OFFER | C. OR NAFF OFF

4. PC Daniels arrested the suspect.

A. PERSONAL COMPUTER | B. POPULAR CAPTAIN | C. POLICE CONSTABLE

5. The FA Cup Final is always held at Wembley Stadium.

A. FOOTBALL ASSOCIATION | B. FINEST ATHLETES | C. FOOTBALL ALLIANCE

6. My GP signed me off work for two days.

A. GOVERNMENT PHYSICIAN | B. GIVER OF PRESCRIPTIONS | C. GENERAL PRACTITIONER

Exercise 2

NAMES FOR PEOPLE FROM AROUND THE UK

Match the people with the place where they're from.

1. A BRUMMIE
2. AN EAST ENDER
3. A GEORDIE
4. A GLASWEGIAN
5. A LONDONER
6. A MACKEM
7. A MANCUNIAN
8. A SCOUSER

A. SOMEONE FROM THE EAST END OF LONDON
B. SOMEONE FROM GLASGOW
C. SOMEONE FROM BIRMINGHAM
D. SOMEONE FROM MANCHESTER
E. SOMEONE FROM NEWCASTLE
F. SOMEONE FROM LONDON
G. SOMEONE FROM LIVERPOOL
H. SOMEONE FROM SUNDERLAND

Exercise 3

EXPRESSIONS WITH ANIMALS

Choose the right animal to complete the phrases.

MONKEY	BEES	DOG (X2)
KITTENS	PONY	ZEBRA
DONKEY	STAG	HEN

1. Can I pay you back next week? I've got no______________ until payday.

   (Cockney rhyming slang for money)

2. This new app is the ______________'s bollocks.

   (a rude phrase to say that something is the best)

3. I haven't been back to my home town in ______________'s years.

   (a long time)

4. Don't tell your parents you're doing a skydive. They'll have ______________!

   (to be very anxious or worried)

5. I got paid a ______________ for repainting that house.

(London slang for £500)

6. Let's not go somewhere expensive. I've only got a ______________ in my pocket.

(London slang for £25)

7. I got myself a job in the shop as a general ______________sbody – stocking shelves, sweeping the floor, that sort of thing.

(a person who is asked to do all the menial tasks and jobs no one else wants to do)

8. Helen's having her ______________ party the weekend before the wedding.

(the celebration a bride has before she gets married)

9. James' best man organised his ______________ do – with a few surprises.

(the celebration a groom has before he gets married)

10. Drivers should stop at the ______________ crossing and let pedestrians cross.

(an area painted white and black across a road, where pedestrians can cross)

Exercise 4

SOMETHING AND SOMETHING

Choose the right word to complete the phrases. All the phrases have the form '______ and ______'.

SODS	EMERGENCY	BLINDING
TATTIES	BOBS	OXBRIDGE
SO	BUTTER	

1. We've almost got everything we need for the barbecue. We just need a few more bits and ______________ but we can get them last-minute.

   (small objects or miscellaneous things. We often use this phrase when it would take too long naming all the things or we don't know the words for them)

2. Did you see the team captain when he got sent off? He started effing and ______________ to the ref!

   (saying swear words)

3. I'd love to become a full-time DJ, but accounting is my bread and ______________.

   (the job that gives you your main income)

4. You lazy so-and-_____________! Why don't you give me a hand once in a while?

(a person who is considered to have a negative characteristic)

5. Neeps and _____________ are the traditional thing to serve with haggis.

(a side dish served with haggis, made of swede and potatoes)

6. An ambulance will take too long to get here. I'd better drive you to A&E myself.

(the accident and _____________ department in a hospital)

7. A – What's in that box over there?
B – Just a few odds and _____________ from my old flat.

(miscellaneous items)

8. Deepak's dream is to get into _____________ , and then become a politician.

(a term used to refer to the universities of Oxford and Cambridge)

Exercise 5

SLANG

Choose the right slang expression for the sentence.

1. Somebody's made a massive ________. We ordered two items but they've delivered 20!

A. KNEES-UP | B. COCK-UP | C. BUST-UP

2. Sam, you look ________. Have you been running?

A. CHUFFED | B. KNACKERED | C. GUTTED

3. Have we run out of milk? I'll just pop out to the ________.

A. CORNER SHOP | B. CHARITY SHOP | C. OFF-LICENCE

4. We don't really need the premium package. Let's just get the ________ one.

A. BOG-STANDARD | B. A-LEVEL | C. FULL MONTY

5. I've got to get out of this pub before the football match starts. I ________ all the shouting and screaming.

A. CAN'T BE DOING WITH | B. CAN'T WAIT FOR | C. HAVE THE HUMP WITH

6. That documentary last night was ________ good. When's the next episode?

A. ACE | B. DODGY | C. DEAD

7. I had to work a 12-hour shift without a proper break. I'm _________!

A. SORTED | B. SHATTERED | C. JAMMY

8. That T-shirt's a bargain. Only costs _________.

A. A MONKEY | B. A GRAND | C. A FIVER

9. I was working on this massive project at work but it all _________ when the buyer pulled out of the deal.

A. WENT DOWN | B. WENT PEAR-SHAPED | C. PISSED OFF

10. I think I passed the exam, _________. I'll get the results next month.

A. MUSTN'T GRUMBLE | B. TOUCH WOOD | C. JOLLY GOOD

11. Can I pay you back next week? I'm absolutely _________ at the moment.

A. ACE | B. MINTED | C. SKINT

12. That area's a bit _________. I wouldn't walk alone round there, especially after dark.

A. DODGY | B. POSH | C. RUBBISH

Exercise 6

FOOD AND DRINK

Use the clues to complete the crossword.

ACROSS

2. A slang term for a cup of tea. Mostly used in the north of England.
5. A long green vegetable ('zucchini' in American English).
6. A slang word for food.
7. A sweet dish served at the end of a meal. Synonym of dessert. The short form is pud.
9. A fish and chip shop.

10. A wild drinking session.
13. The evening meal. Used mainly in the north of England.
15. A term used mostly in the north of England for sandwich.
16. A building in which alcohol is sold and consumed. Short for public house.
18. A greasy _________ is a cheap and cheerful cafe that sells mainly fried food.
20. A _________ pudding is a traditional side dish eaten with a Sunday roast, made of batter consisting of eggs, flour, and milk or water.
22. A break in the late morning in which one might have a coffee or light snack. It's usually around 11 o'clock.

DOWN

1. A type of fizzy alcoholic drink that usually comes in fruity flavours.
3. A full _________ breakfast is a traditional breakfast usually consisting of sausages, eggs, bacon, baked beans, tomatoes, mushrooms, black pudding, and toast.

4. An informal term for vegetarian.
8. A wobbly sweet fruity dessert ('jell-o' in American English).
9. Short for a cup of tea.
11. An adjective to describe food that is heavy and filling.
12. Feeling very full because you've eaten a lot of food.
14. A large purple vegetable ('eggplant' in American English).
15. A sausage.
16. A small container that holds fruit.
17. _________ fizz is an alcoholic drink made with orange and champagne.
19. Short for vegetables.
21. An alcoholic drink of beer mixed with lemonade.

Exercise 7

THE GREAT BRITISH QUIZ

1. What is the second biggest city in Britain by population?

A. EDINBURGH | B. MANCHESTER | C. BIRMINGHAM

2. Who is the patron saint of Wales?

A. ST ANDREW | B. ST JOHN | C. ST DAVID

3. Who lives at Number 10 Downing Street?

A. THE KING | B. THE PRIME MINISTER | C. DAVID BECKHAM

4. What year did London most recently host the summer Olympic Games?

A. 1948 | B. 2012 | C. 2016

5. Which famous London landmark is actually the name of the bell, not the tower?

A. TOWER BRIDGE | B. BIG BEN | C. THE SHARD

6. What is the longest running British soap opera on TV?

A. EMMERDALE | B. CORONATION STREET | C. EASTENDERS

7. Where is the highest point in Great Britain?

A. SNOWDON (OR YR WYDDFA) | B. BEN NEVIS | C. HOLME FEN

8. What is the name of the British flag?

A. UNION JOHN | B. UNION JIM | C. UNION JACK

9. Who is next in line to the throne?

A. PRINCE WILLIAM | B. PRINCE HARRY | C. PRINCE GEORGE

10. Which team plays their football matches at Anfield?

A. LIVERPOOL | B. MANCHESTER UNITED | C. WEST HAM UNITED

11. Which king established the Church of England?

A. GEORGE V | B. HENRY VIII | C. JAMES II

12. How old do you have to be to receive a personalised birthday card from the King?

A. 1 | B. 50 | C. 100

13. What is the tallest building in the United Kingdom?

A. THE GHERKIN | B. THE SHARD | C. CANARY WHARF (ONE CANADA SQUARE)

14. Which British national doesn't need a passport?

A. THE KING | B. THE PRIME MINISTER | C. THE FOREIGN MINISTER

15. What is the legal drinking age in the UK?

A. 16 | B. 18 | C. 21

16. What is the longest river in Britain?

A. THE THAMES | B. THE TRENT | C. THE SEVERN

17. What accent comes from Newcastle?

A. COCKNEY | B. GEORDIE | C. SCOUSE

18. In what year did the United Kingdom vote to leave the European Union (Brexit referendum)?

A. 2014 | B. 2016 | C. 2018

19. Who was the first female British Prime Minister?

A. MARGARET THATCHER | B. THERESA MAY | C. HARRIET HARMAN

20. What is the name of the travelling Scottish football fans?

A. HAGGIS ARMY | B. NESS ARMY | C. TARTAN ARMY

ANSWERS

EXERCISE 1

1. a 2. c 3. b 4. c 5. a 6. c

EXERCISE 2

1. c 2. a 3. e 4. b 5. f 6. h 7. d 8. g

EXERCISE 3

1. bees 2. dog 3. donkey 4. kittens 5. monkey 6. pony 7. dog 8. hen 9. stag 10. zebra

EXERCISE 4

1. bobs 2. blinding 3. butter 4. so 5. tattoos 6. emergency 7. sods 8. Oxbridge

EXERCISE 5

1. b 2. b 3. a 4. a 5. a 6. c 7. b 8. c 9. b 10. b 11. c 12. a

EXERCISE 6

Across

2. brew
5. courgette
6. grub
7. pudding
9. chippy
10. bender
13. tea
15. butty
16. pub
18. spoon
20. Yorkshire
22. elevenses

Down

1. alcopop
3. English
4. veggie
8. jelly
9. cuppa
11. stodgy
12. stuffed
14. aubergine
15. banger
16. punnet
17. buck's
19. veg
21. shandy

EXERCISE 7

1. Birmingham
2. St David
3. The Prime Minister
4. 2012
5. Big Ben
6. Coronation Street
7. Ben Nevis
8. Union Jack
9. Prince William
10. Liverpool
11. Henry VIII
12. 100
13. The Shard
14. The King
15. 18
16. The Severn
17. Geordie
18. 2016
19. Margaret Thatcher
20. Tartan Army